C000134260

On:
The Essence
of Time

Essays on Mastering the Shortness of Life.

A Tribute to Seneca

by

Robert N. Jacobs

Grosvenor House
Publishing Limited

All rights reserved
Copyright © Robert N. Jacobs, 2024

The right of Robert N. Jacobs to be identified as the author of this
work has been asserted in accordance with Section 78
of the Copyright, Designs and Patents Act 1988

The book cover is copyright to Robert N. Jacobs

This book is published by
Grosvenor House Publishing Ltd
Link House
140 The Broadway, Tolworth, Surrey, KT6 7HT.
www.grosvenorhousepublishing.co.uk

This book is sold subject to the conditions that it shall not, by way of
trade or otherwise, be lent, resold, hired out or otherwise circulated
without the author's or publisher's prior consent in any form of
binding or cover other than that in which it is published and
without a similar condition including this condition being
imposed on the subsequent purchaser.

A CIP record for this book
is available from the British Library

ISBN 978-1-80381-818-4

"It is not that we have a short time to live, but that we waste a lot of it. Life is long enough, and a sufficiently generous amount has been given to us for the highest achievements if it were all well invested. But when it is wasted in heedless luxury and spent on no good activity, we are forced at last by death's final constraint to realise that it has passed away before we knew it was passing. So it is: we are not given a short life, but we make it short, and we are not ill-supplied but wasteful of it. Life is long if you know how to use it."

Seneca, On the Shortness of Life, 49AD

Acknowledgements

This book is lovingly dedicated to my beloved wife, Simona, and our precious daughter, Ava. They are the radiant beacon in my life; their love, wisdom, and unwavering support have been my driving force in completing this work. Their strength infuses me daily, for which I am profoundly thankful. Additionally, my heartfelt gratitude goes to my parents, who laid a solid foundation from my earliest years, providing a platform for me to flourish.

Robert N. Jacobs

Foreword

For me, time is one of the few powerful man-made concepts that I believe do not exist in nature but nonetheless shape our lives. Similar notions include the existence of various gods, Santa Claus, and the Easter Bunny. All were conceived by man. All have profound effects on us. All were generated for good reason.

Of course, many more humans believe in time than any of the others, which makes time the motherboard of the human story. It is against time that all human achievement, progress, and change is measured. I wonder what they did before they invented sundials in Mesopotamia in 3500 BCE?

As a species, humans have a compelling need for certainty, to understand our environment, and to explain life. This is why a variety of dominant human fictions have arisen. Each is an attempt to help us shape our understanding and behaviour in ways perceived to be 'better' by the authors. Each brings both benefit and misery. Like all tools, they can be used for good or evil.

Time brings us the ability to organise our lives, to benchmark ourselves and to judge others. Without it, we could not be 'early', 'ageing' or 'living in the moment'. We would have no safe competitive sport. There would be no speed. Productivity could not exist. There would be no calendar. No SMART goals. No future. No past. No today. No tomorrow. No birthdays. Much less stress. Life as we think of it today would simply not exist.

So, while time itself may be a fiction, its impact is real and impactful, and just like other human constructs like politics and money, we ignore it at our peril. Those who master the story can gain an advantage in the competitive game of life we have created for our species. Time is the artificial pitch on which we all play the game of life.

When we play a game, we either play to win or to enjoy playing. Playing to win sets you on a course of maximising the gain from every second spent on the pitch, planning for what lies ahead and valuing each moment from its investment potential and likely return. It is the destination or end goal that drives us.

Playing to play leads you more to maximising the consumption returns in the moment while doing enough to stay in the game. It is the journey that drives us.

As I reflect on my own life at 61 years old, I sense I have been mainly in my own way hanging on inside the game and enjoying it while setting myself modest goals to attain en route. Others have won Olympic Gold, made Billions, or brought the world to emotional highs or lows.

As a baby, I was oblivious to the notion of time, as a child it seemed unimportant and I sensed it passed slowly. Today it seems to be that everything zips by and is lost in a flash. As Pink Floyd famously penned... 'And then one day you find, ten years have got behind you. No one told you when to run; you missed the starting gun.'

I hope that you find the different perspectives of time discussed, expressed, and shared in these pages worthy of your time, whether you believe that they exist or not!

A.L.J. Pratt OBE JP FRSA FIOD

Table of Contents

Introduction

It was late in the day, and the sun's light was starting to fade. A brisk wind blew through the city streets and a chill settled in. It had been a long day, and it wasn't even close to being over yet. John, an elderly man who lived alone in the city, started to feel like life was slipping away from him. He felt as though his life had been too short. The years seemed to have passed by quickly, and he had not accomplished what he wanted in them. He knew that he was running out of time, and he hadn't done enough. He remembered the days when he was younger and full of energy, but now those days were gone forever. He thought back to all that he had accomplished over the years – all that he wanted to do but never got around too – and his heart ached with regret and sadness.

This book aims to help you avoid the regrets that John felt. Growing older can be a bittersweet experience. We are often comforted by the knowledge that we have made good choices and done things we can look back on with pride, but alas, it is the things that we failed to do, or didn't try hard enough at that haunt us in our later years. We may learn to regret not having taken risks and not having embraced opportunities when they were presented to us. It's only in old age that we realise there are few second chances; life goes on regardless of whether we seize it.

In the words of the great Roman philosopher Seneca, *"Life is short, so don't waste it."*

This is a sentiment that has been echoed throughout human history, and one that has been particularly relevant in recent times. In a world where life is continually accelerating and filled with technological advancements, the notion of life being too short has taken on a new meaning. People are living longer than ever before, but their lives feel increasingly shorter.

This book explores the philosophy of Seneca and its relevance to our modern lives as we struggle to battle against the waning sense of time. Though Seneca lived over two millennia ago, his teachings remain as relevant today as they were then. He understood how precious life was and he encouraged people to make the most of every moment.

He understood that life was too short to be wasted on pursuits that did not bring joy or enrich the mind. He believed that everyone should strive for excellence in all areas of their lives – both physical and emotional – so that each day could be approached with enthusiasm and passion. The fact remains: life is too short to be taken lightly. Everyone must make sure they live every day purposefully and with respect for those around them.

Many have found solace in Seneca's teachings. He provided an alternative perspective on how people should live based on a timeless understanding of what truly matters in life: wisdom, love, and friendship. Seneca had a clear view of priorities for time management and spending time wisely. He argued that while it is important to focus on long-term goals such as career growth or financial stability, it is equally important to enjoy each moment as if it were your last – because you may not get another chance! In other words, don't get caught up in worry about what could happen tomorrow. Instead, enjoy what you have now and take steps toward making tomorrow even better than today.

Life may be short, but if you make wise choices and use your time wisely, it will be long enough. You can experience joy and contentment in moments, if you choose to savour the little things that otherwise pass by too quickly. When you spend time engaging with meaningful experiences and relationships, life can be wonderful, no matter how fleeting.

No matter how much or how little time you have, life will always be what you make of it, so use your moments wisely knowing that life is a precious gift to make the most of. We have the power to make our limited time feel much longer than it is if we use every second wisely.

Finally, this is not a typical book that transitions smoothly from one chapter to the next. Instead, it's an anthology of essays, each with its own distinctive charm. Each one should be read with a thoughtful mindset, pondered upon, and analysed before moving on to the next. Let's embrace the ancient wisdom and journey through the pages together, exploring how Seneca's lessons can be relevant in today's world.

Chapter 1

Life is Finite

In the small town of Colby, there lived an old man who went by the name of Oliver. He was content with his life and rarely left his house except to gather a few groceries at the local market.

Oliver had a routine that he stuck to every day, but one day his idyllic routine all came crashing down. He suddenly fell ill and ended up in hospital, where he was surrounded by medical staff working around the clock. He watched as they worked and filled their time helping people and he couldn't shake off the feeling that there were still things he hadn't accomplished in his own life.

As he lay in bed for days on end, regrets filled his mind. He realised just how limited his time on this Earth truly was. He knew then that no matter how long he had to live, it would never be enough. Every moment should be cherished so that he didn't miss out on making meaningful memories or accomplishing his goals.

The old man eventually recovered from his illness and returned home with newfound wisdom about life and its fragility. Instead of wasting any more time feeling regretful over what he could have done differently, he started living each day as if it was his last, making plans and going out of his way to make others smile. For Oliver, Seneca's words had come alive: "Don't live as if you have unlimited time."

Back in his home, he vowed that he would remember Seneca's wise words whenever faced with difficult decisions or seemingly mundane tasks, because you never know when your time may run out.

Impermanence

You can no more control the flow of time than you can control the ebb and swell of the sea. Everything around you change and moves; nothing ever truly remains still. Oliver had no control over his sudden illness and the need to be hospitalised. His life changed suddenly, and happenings were out with his control. Not everything is within our control, and there is impermanence in all things, including change itself. Use this knowledge to help you focus on the present, make the most of every moment, and embrace and learn from change and the opportunities it brings.

The morbid thought of death often casts a dark shadow over our existence. But rather than bemoaning the fact that we are mortal, perhaps we should learn to accept it and live with death. Seneca knew this and suggested that peace in life could only be achieved once mortality had been acknowledged. He saw death not as a tragedy, but as a chance to ensure we live meaningful lives while connecting deeply with those around us. This was something he personally strived toward in his own life, knowing full well that his time was finite. Knowing that existence is transitory should not be a cause for worry, it should instead motivate you to make your life rich and full each day.

If you focus too much on what has passed or what will come, you will miss out on the beauty that resides in every moment of living. You should therefore be mindful of mortality, without dwelling on it, recognising impermanence as an advantage and a blessing that lights your way in life. Oliver's reflections and regrets motivated him to behave differently. He vowed to cherish every moment, make meaningful memories, and accomplish his goals.

Seneca believed that the beauty of life lay in its impermanence. It is up to us to take full advantage of every moment we have. We must strive to find joy in the little things and be grateful for our blessings, however fleeting they may be. Let us embrace change with open arms, knowing that even if something passes away, it can still bring new lessons and opportunities into our lives. Oliver learned about mortality and how to value his remaining time on Earth after his experience of illness and hospitalisation. The change he experienced brought him the opportunity to enjoy his life and live it more meaningfully. Life is precious: let us not waste a single day!

We should take comfort in the fact that whatever happens – whether good or bad – it will eventually pass. Difficult times will come and go, as will moments of delight and pleasure. No matter what challenges we may face, we must remember that there is always light at the end of the tunnel. Life may be unpredictable and ever-changing, but this should not stop us from living it to the fullest.

Accept your mortality and live a meaningful life. Accept change and that difficult times will come and go. Focus on the present. Make each day rich, taking full advantage of every moment by using them for meaningful activities that will bring you joy.

Precious Moments

We need to make every moment count by treasuring the little things in life, such as time spent with our loved ones and moments of peace when we can reflect on the beauty around us. It's important to find joy in each day, no matter how small or seemingly insignificant the source of that joy may be. This will help us be mindful of living in the present instead of worrying about what may come.

It's important to be brave and take risks that will lead to personal growth and fulfilment – after all, life is too short not to try something new. Words of wisdom passed down through the centuries encourage this: *"It is not because things are difficult that we do not dare; it is because we do not dare that they are difficult."* We should strive for balance between work and leisure activities, seeking out experiences that bring us joy and help to look after our mental well-being. We should have goals, but we should also know that if a goal requires too much effort or is no longer in line with our values, it's okay to let it go.

Above all, we should cherish every moment we have by living life to the fullest: who knows what tomorrow may bring? In the story above, Oliver took his life for granted and only when it changed did he learn how much there was to appreciate. By making the most of each day, we can guarantee that no matter how unpredictable life may be, we will still make the most of it.

Focusing on what is within our control – the present moment – can help us channel resources toward creating more meaningful relationships and making better use of our time. Treasure even the smallest pleasures, be brave enough to explore new things, find activities you enjoy to lead a full and meaningful life, and let go of the activities that fail to fulfil.

Regrets

Thich Nhat Hanh explained, *"When our minds are free from worries about the future and regrets about the past, we experience real happiness in each moment of being alive."* We all have regrets and moments we would prefer hadn't happened. If we could go back and change what we did or the outcome of an event, we would, given the chance. Oliver regretted the way he had spent his life, but it was part of his story and served as a way for him to learn a valuable lesson. Reflecting on what we could have done differently – or better – can help us in the future. We can apply what we have learned to our future decisions and behaviour.

Reflecting, however, is not dwelling. Rather than dwell on past mistakes, focus instead on finding ways to make better use of time. This may not necessarily mean working longer hours, but rather being more mindful of how you spend your time, ensuring it is productive and meaningful. Consider the activities that bring you joy and set aside time for these things as well as your work. This can help balance out the feelings of regret while still allowing progress to be made.

Take heart from the knowledge that we all make mistakes, and recognise that what we learn from our mistakes helps us to develop resilience and wisdom. By letting go of regret while striving to live with intent, we can create a life filled with joy and purpose. So, take heart, be brave, and make the most of every moment.

Procrastination

There may have been many reasons for Oliver not achieving more in his life prior to his illness, but one of those reasons was likely to have been procrastination. Seneca argued, *"Life is too short to waste away in procrastination; instead let us take action and pursue our goals!"*

Procrastination is an all too familiar enemy of progress. It plagues us with guilt, regret, and wasted potential. It's a natural instinct for some, and for others it can be a learned behaviour that's difficult to overcome. The desire to delay or put off tasks arises from multiple sources including simple laziness, perfectionism, fear of failure or success, lack of knowledge and experience with the task at hand, or low confidence in our abilities. In addition to these reasons, procrastination can indicate a larger problem such as poor decision-making skills or difficulty handling stress, which should also be addressed.

Putting an end to procrastination starts with identifying what your self-disruptive patterns are. Ask yourself why you are putting off a given task or activity and what underlying cause is stopping you from getting started. Once you have identified why you are procrastinating, you will find it easy to develop strategies to overcome the problem and develop more productive habits.

A practical strategy for avoiding procrastination is to break down large tasks into smaller, more manageable parts which can be completed more easily than the whole task. Establishing specific timelines for completing the subtasks with realistic goals will help you to keep motivated. You will become focused on completing the subtasks in an organised manner, instead of putting the whole task aside indefinitely. Further, you can reward yourself when you meet these smaller goals; this creates positive reinforcement. Each achievement rewarded helps motivate continued progression and productivity.

Challenging work can often be daunting and overwhelming so it's only natural to feel like giving up at times, especially when you find yourself struggling to stay on task. With patience and perseverance, tasks can and will eventually become easier. Taking regular breaks from work can also help you to re-energise and remain productive for longer.

Developing supportive habits and routines will help you to stay consistent and on target to achieve your goals. Sticking to routines makes it harder for procrastination to take hold, since a set structure is already established for completing tasks on time. Furthermore, by scheduling specific blocks of time throughout the day for working on particular tasks, you will be more likely to persevere and avoid procrastination.

Procrastination can have negative consequences on your life if not addressed properly. If you tend to procrastinate, identify why, and make a few adjustments to your habits and routines. This will help you to overcome procrastination and make the most of your time. By breaking down large tasks into smaller chunks, setting realistic goals with rewards for completion, taking regular breaks from work, and establishing supportive routines, you will progress toward greater personal fulfilment without falling prey to procrastination, the enemy of progress.

Self-Awareness

Self-awareness is the key to unlocking true fulfilment. Through self-reflection, we can uncover what activities make us feel good and which ones have a negative impact on our mood. This knowledge allows us to prioritise certain tasks or hobbies so that we can focus our energy on what truly enriches our lives, rather than just wasting time on things that cause frustration or boredom. This is precisely what happened to Oliver in hospital. He reflected on his life, and the new knowledge he discovered about himself and the life he had led helped him to refocus on what might truly enrich his life from that point onwards.

Having a deeper awareness of ourselves helps clarify how we want to spend our time and energy. We can actively seek out experiences that are meaningful, such as spending quality time with loved ones or engaging in pursuits that bring us joy. By taking the time to understand what truly brings us fulfilment, we gain a greater appreciation of life and its moments of beauty.

Additionally, being aware of our strengths and weaknesses helps us to be more honest with ourselves and others. We learn how to accept who we are and where we come from, while also recognising areas in which we need improvement so that these can be addressed over time. With this understanding of ourselves comes greater confidence, allowing us to better stand up for our beliefs and take risks to pursue our passions.

Self-awareness is essential for anyone looking to achieve true fulfilment in their lifetime. Through knowledge of what we find meaningful, what makes us happy, and our strengths and weaknesses, we can be more mindful of how we choose to use our time, so that each day brings us closer to contentment and peace.

Strength of Mind

Seneca believed that having a strong mind was a great benefit to living well: *"It is not a weak mind that endures storms and overcomes them; it is the strong mind that knows how to turn every change in its favour."* Though life may sometimes bring unexpected experiences, wise and resolute minds are able to adapt and react with courage and composure. Oliver experienced his illness and consequent hospital stay as his life "crashing down" whereas in truth, it was an opportunity for him to self-reflect and redirect his energies; a chance to adapt.

In times of uncertainty, it is important to stop and ponder the best course of action, while being mindful that situations can change quickly. Remaining patient and unrushed but taking decisive action requires a balancing act. Informed by experience or advice from trusted peers, you should strive for deliberate thoughtfulness in your response to any given set of circumstances.

A beneficial strategy for responding wisely to unexpected circumstances involves identifying opportunities within the challenge itself. In this way, embracing difficulty becomes an avenue for growth rather than something to dread or avoid. Taking advantage of these moments requires an optimistic mindset; an attitude of looking ahead at what can be gained instead of fixating on what has been lost. While this outlook may take some practice, developing resilience allows progress – no matter what comes your way. With time, Oliver may have come to learn that what frightened him, and the change in his life, was nothing to be afraid of. It was something he could meet with courage, while embracing the opportunity it brought to improve his life.

It is also essential to recognise that you are unlikely to be able to respond effectively alone. Humility and determination go hand in hand, and humbly seeking assistance from those you trust will deliver results much faster than if you battle on alone. The perspectives of others will help you resolve issues and plan how to proceed. This approach yields greater rewards and cultivates healthy social networks that benefit everyone.

No matter what life throws at you, keeping strong in mind and responding wisely to unexpected circumstances with calmness and confidence will lead you toward positive outcomes that enrich you on your journey through life.

When faced with sudden variations in routine or disappointments when life falls short of your expectations, strive to strengthen your mind and remain prepared for whatever is around the next corner. Be ready to accept each moment, whatever it brings, make decisions calmly, ask others for help, and look for opportunities.

Excellence

Success is not achieved by striving for perfection, but rather by striving for excellence. When you strive for excellence instead of perfection, you open yourself up to greater potential for success. Striving for perfection can overwhelm and demotivate you.

Achieving excellence requires balance. While it is important to challenge yourself to reach greatness and lead a meaningful life, it is also important to forgive yourself when things don't turn out perfectly. Be kind to yourself along this journey. Part of what makes us human is our imperfections, so keep persevering despite inevitable failures or shortcomings along the way. Don't see failure or imperfection as something negative or bad, but as an opportunity to learn and grow.

Rather than trying to achieve some unattainable ideal of perfection, set small achievable goals that will allow incremental progress towards excellence. Celebrate the small victories along the way and keep pushing forward, even when faced with adversity and setbacks. Approach any task with curiosity instead of apprehension; explore new angles, gain understanding from different perspectives, and widen your scope to prompt fresh ideas rather than becoming content with mediocrity.

There are many ways to reach success in whatever you are doing. Ask questions, seek advice from those who have gone before you or those around you now, take up challenges that push your boundaries one step further each time, but don't forget that it all starts inside. Trust in your capacity and capabilities while being mindful of how far you are willing to stretch yourself. Don't push yourself so hard that you break down entirely.

Striving for excellence rather than perfection requires self-awareness and dedication. Success doesn't equate to perfect execution but to a better understanding. Let go of fear of failure and permit yourself to explore without judgment or expectation so that you can ultimately work toward achieving greatness, instead of striving idly toward perfectionism's false alure. Let go of the dream of perfection and be kind to yourself; forgive your failures and celebrate small victories.

Focus

It can be challenging to remain focused on meaningful tasks when the world constantly bombards you with distractions. We are no longer able to find solace in the serenity of stillness. We are endlessly assaulted with notifications from our phones or advertisements on television and streaming services. When constantly faced with distractions, don't despair! Simply work harder at maintaining your presence of mind. The greatest obstacle to getting things done lies within you.

Our minds can be like a crowded room with too many conversations going on at once. We need to learn how to shut out some of those conversations to save time and mental energy.

Mindfulness practices such as meditation and journaling allow us to tap into clarity. Meditation helps free your mind from unnecessary chatter, allowing you to take a momentary break from the constant hustle and bustle of life. Likewise, journaling helps organise thought processes, allowing for greater clarity and insight when approaching various tasks. Through activities such as these, you can cultivate peace of mind, and with peace of mind, it will become apparent to you why you need to prioritise meaningful tasks over mindless distracting indulgences.

Not only does focusing on what matters help you to become more productive, it also leads to a more relaxed state so you can enjoy moments without being constantly peppered by irrelevant information. By focusing your energy on worthwhile goals instead of succumbing to the noise around you, you will become better equipped to take conscious steps toward achieving the objectives that truly matter to you in your life. Perhaps Oliver's quiet time in hospital without work or other distractions gave him the opportunity to realise what activities were truly important to him in life.

Life shouldn't be lived as a collection of multitasking activities with never-ending lists of things to do. Life should be an adventure, where mindful presence is savoured and enjoyed. Life shouldn't be rushed through hurriedly, and needless distractions shouldn't be holding us back or leading us off track. Don't give in to the onslaught of modern-day disturbances. Set aside time for mindful practices that bring clarity, so that you can prioritise what truly matters most in your life today.

Courage and Gratitude

We live in a world of uncertainty: the future is never certain. We can make plans for tomorrow, but we can never be sure that our plans will play out. This uncertainty makes it difficult to live with courage and purpose, and often leads us to feel a sense of anxiety or fear.

Seneca pointed out the value of courage: *"Staunchness of mind and courage will enable one to go through life with a steady step and an unruffled spirit."* With courage and mental fortitude, neither good nor bad fortune will overwhelm you, and you will anticipate and accept both with equanimity. Courage allows us to face our hardships bravely rather than shrink away from them in fear or despair. Seneca believed that *it is not because things are difficult that we do not dare, it is because we do not dare that they are difficult.* Having courage and awareness enables us to make decisions which lead to a better future.

Gratitude allows you to recognise how even seemingly small events shape your life, such as a kind word here or an unexpected helping hand there. As you move toward your goal, appreciate everything, and celebrate both the small successes and the larger ones that come your way.

In summary, living with courage means facing life's challenges bravely, and practicing gratitude lets you appreciate even small victories along the way.

A Purposeful, Meaningful Life

"A man should always have these two rules in readiness: to do nothing without purpose, and to do nothing without meaning." Seneca warned about wasting our limited days on small matters, emphasising that all of our activities should have meaning and bring satisfaction. If you always keep this in mind, then every moment can become precious and worthwhile, regardless of how long you have left on this Earth.

One way to ensure that each day has purpose is to set yourself goals and then work hard (but in a smart way) to achieve them. Your goal might be to develop a new skill or improve yourself in some way, contribute positively to society, pursue hobbies, spend quality time with family and friends, look after your physical health, educate yourself about important issues, explore meaningful concepts or ideas, live generously and help others where possible, or embrace cultural experiences. Without purpose, we are directionless. While it may take some time to discover, everyone has a specific purpose that gives them drive and direction, or a destination toward which all their actions should be moving.

Knowing your purpose demystifies many of the difficulties we face on our journey through life; it helps us prioritise tasks and understand when something is worth striving for despite the struggle associated with achieving it.

Seneca argued that success itself is not important. What matters most is our happiness and contentment within the context of a larger mission or vision, which is understanding our place in the world by staying true to ourselves and trying to do right by those around us regardless of the outcome. It doesn't matter if your goals are insignificant or grandiose. What makes them worthwhile is the effort you put into their achievement.

Seneca's lesson here is to find contentment through identifying what has meaning to you and will make you happy. Knowing your meaningful purpose means you can set yourself meaningful goals, which you are motivated to strive toward. Whether you succeed is irrelevant; the effort you make toward them will bring you happiness and contentment. As Seneca argued: *"Life is short – let us fill it up with deeds worthy of remembrance!"* Let us find joy in whatever time we have left here on Earth. After all, it's what we choose to do with it that will determine its worthiness.

Lessons from Life is Finite

Accept your mortality and live a meaningful life. Accept change and that difficult times will come and go. Focus on the present. Make each day rich, taking full advantage of every moment, using them for meaningful activities that will bring you joy.

Treasure even the smallest pleasures, be brave in exploring new things, find activities you enjoy to lead a full and meaningful life, and let go of the activities that fail to fulfil.

Let go of regret and live with intent to create a life filled with joy and purpose. We all make mistakes but what we learn from our mistakes helps us to develop resilience and wisdom.

Procrastination is the enemy of progress. If you tend to procrastinate, identify why, and make a few adjustments to establish supportive routines.

Self-awareness will help you find true fulfilment in your lifetime. Through knowledge of what you find meaningful, what makes you happy, and your strengths and weaknesses, you can be more mindful of how you choose to use your time so that each day brings you closer to contentment and peace.

No matter what life throws at you, keep strong in mind. Accept each moment, whatever it brings, make decisions calmly, ask others for help, and look for opportunities.

Let go of the dream of perfection and be kind to yourself; forgive your failures and celebrate small victories.

Keep focused. Don't give in to the onslaught of modern-day disturbances. Set aside time for mindful practices that bring clarity so that you can prioritise what truly matters most in your life.

Live with courage, face life's challenges bravely, and be grateful for even small victories along the way.

Chapter 2

Living in the Moment

Once upon a time, there was a young man named Marcus who lived his life as the wind blew. He felt that nothing was so important that it couldn't wait until tomorrow. If a friend called by, inviting him to a party, he would go along. If someone phoned for a chat, he would chat, and if he became bored working on something, he would pick up his phone and scroll through Instagram postings to see what his friends had been up to at the weekend.

Marcus became bitter in life as his friends began to get exciting jobs, follow their dream courses, or find the love of their lives to marry. He failed at his studies, his work was always only ever temporary, and he had nobody he cared for a great deal in his life.

One day, one of his friends invited him to his wedding. At the wedding, Marcus grew bored and started scrolling through his phone. The groom came up to him and asked him what he was doing. Marcus told him he had grown bored sitting on his own at the wedding, and that he wasn't lucky like his friend. He had nobody to dance with.

"Is that what you really want in life, Marcus? To meet someone to dance with, to enjoy life with, to get to know, and to eventually love?"

"Yes, of course, but it hasn't happened to me like it has to you. You're lucky."

"It isn't all luck, my friend. Here you are, sitting amongst all these good people you could be introducing yourself to. You aren't present in the moment. You are distracted with your phone and friends who aren't here with you. Seize the moment, dear friend! Life is not for eternity! Go and ask one of these people to dance with you. That's the first small step to meeting someone you can love. And it's totally within your control."

The groom left Marcus alone again. Marcus thought about what his friend had said and looked around the room. He asked someone to dance, and two years later, he married that person.

After that day, Marcus lived according to one simple principle: avoid distractions. He had seen far too many people become slaves to their short-term desires and passions, losing sight of what really mattered in life – living in the moment.

Marcus realised that by avoiding distractions, he could truly appreciate and savour life's precious moments. To him, being distracted meant missing out on the beauty of living in each present moment. Later in life, he would often tell people, "Don't let your mind be disturbed by anything that can take you away from the present."

To achieve this level of focus, Marcus adopted a lifestyle of mindfulness and self-control. He practiced meditation daily and kept his body healthy through exercise and healthy eating. Whenever he encountered temptations or distractions, he calmly analysed them, and consciously chose to ignore them if they did not contribute to his overall goals in life.

To remain focused while juggling multiple tasks at once, Marcus also utilised a unique technique called 'mental refocusing'. This technique allowed him to switch between different tasks with ease by keeping his primary goal always at the front of his mind.

In our modern lives, it's easy to become distracted by technology, social media, or any number of external influences, but if we practice mindful techniques like those used by Marcus, we can stay focused on embracing each moment as it comes without letting ourselves get sidetracked by fleeting distractions.

Impacts of Distraction

Distraction has become an all-pervasive force in our lives, leading us away from what matters most. We have all experienced the pull of technology and social media, and how it completely absorbs us, preventing us from tending to our own needs and to connections with others. If we could learn to recognise the power that distraction holds over us and better understand its effect on our lives, we would be more firmly grounded in reality and ready for whatever life throws at us. Understanding the effects of distractions on your life is key if you want to turn away from them to focus on aspects that hold true significance for you.

Distraction can lead to feelings of inadequacy, unhappiness, and lack of motivation due to the lack of focus on meaningful tasks. When distracted, we lose sight of the bigger picture and are unable to properly prioritise objectives and goals. This can lead to unfinished projects or tasks, resulting in wasted time and energy, and unfulfilled ambitions.

We need to take responsibility for our actions by taking control of how we respond to the temptations of distractions, and thereby live life with purpose and intention. We have limited capacity for attention compared with other living creatures, so we must appreciate how important focusing our attention is and use our time wisely. By choosing an activity intentionally, we avoid falling prey to the temptation of activities which perhaps engage us fleetingly but distract us from achieving our goals. After his friend had talked to him, Marcus made a conscious decision to ask someone to dance with him. He took responsibility for his actions. He controlled his behaviour. By focusing on something related to one of his goals in life, he moved a step closer to achieving it.

Gaining a deeper understanding of how distraction affects us helps us to make decisions that support rather than hinder success. By identifying patterns of behaviour or thought that are not aligned with personal ambitions, we can refocus on our ultimate purpose in life.

Time-Wasting Activities

We often participate in activities or conversations that have little or no value, and we can very quickly adopt time-wasting habits. In this fast-paced and technology-driven world, it is easy to be distracted by trivial activities. We can easily find ourselves mindlessly scrolling through social media or watching television – activities that do not contribute to our overall purpose of living a life filled with meaning. Though these activities require little effort, they use up precious time that could otherwise be spent engaging in activities that actually bring us joy and satisfaction. It is important to recognise the power of these distractions as they can take up valuable moments that could instead be used for creative projects or for connecting with loved ones. It is important to recognise when you are wasting your time on trivial pursuits so that you can redirect your focus toward things that really matter to you. This requires discipline.

Understanding that time is a finite resource is essential to properly direct our lives. If you are mindful of the brevity of life, you will focus more on purposeful endeavours, rather than on those which don't bring true happiness or fulfilment. Recognising the fleeting nature of life often serves as an impetus for creating meaningful experiences filled with depth and thoughtfulness, rather than engaging in mindless activities with meaningless outcomes. Once you understand how quickly time passes, you can begin to look critically at how you spend your moments and make more meaningful choices that ultimately help you to live a life with intention, rather than simply behaving as though your activities are entirely predetermined by external forces.

Learning how to prioritise tasks appropriately to avoid time-wasting activities will help you lead a more productive life. The sooner you recognise how trivial activities waste precious time, the more satisfying your life will become. The challenge lies in being able to separate those activities that offer immediate gratification from those that provide greater rewards over a longer period of time. Developing the self-awareness necessary for distinguishing between these two types of activities is essential for achieving success in any endeavour you pursue. Participating in activities that tap into your passions and desires, rather than relying on external distractions, helps foster a sense of wellbeing and satisfaction from within.

Learn to distinguish between the activities that contribute toward your meaningful goals and those that distract you from them. Acknowledge the brevity of life, and take control over mindless, time-consuming distractions. Instead, direct your time and efforts toward meaningful occupations that enrich your life.

One Day at a Time

Seneca recommended living one day at a time, particularly in the midst of life's constant changes, and that we should live life with gratitude, appreciating each moment. It's foolish to worry too much about the future since life is fleeting, so it's best to focus on what's happening right now. It's also foolish to live in the past with regrets and sorrow. To practice living one day at a time means recognising the gifts present in our lives today and taking advantage of them.

Seneca also wrote about learning and consciously assimilating the lessons from each day as there is much knowledge to be gained through observation and experience. For instance, you can learn how to spot behavioural patterns by observing other people. This might provide insight into your own behaviours and decisions or help you to understand why something happens or doesn't happen.

According to Seneca, being grateful is another important aspect of living one day at a time. Express thanks for all the positive things in life. This will help you to stay grounded and connected with your surroundings. We must be grateful for everything we have, even when times are tough. You will find that you can always find something to appreciate every day.

Ultimately, living in the moment brings us closer to the truth: no matter how hard we try to control our lives, they will never turn out exactly as planned, but if we apply the one day at a time mindset, every second will count and there is always something positive to be thankful for.

Focusing on now, rather than dwelling on regrets of the past or worries of the future, allows us to accept that life's events are sometimes out of our control. We can't always control the outcome, but we can always find the positives in any outcome because there is always something to learn and something to be grateful for in every day of our lives.

Thought Awareness

Seneca taught us that concentration relies on being undistracted by external stimuli and emotions that cloud our perception of reality. In the pursuit of living a meaningful life, it's essential to maintain a clear mind free of mental clutter. This involves assessing your thoughts and evaluating their impact on your ability to concentrate and stay present. Seneca encouraged his followers to free themselves from any afflictions that could hinder clear thinking, such as worrying about things that cannot be changed or that should not be focused on in the moment. Noticing when thoughts become an obstacle can be challenging, but is necessary to move forward with clarity of purpose. Taking a moment to assess what contributes to your mental chaos can provide insight into the weaker links in your thought processes and help you focus better.

Maintaining awareness is key to recognising when distraction-causing anxiety or stress are impinging on your ability to think clearly, leading you to stray away from your purposeful path. Becoming aware of this mental noise allows you greater control over it, so you can remain steadfast in your concentration. To cultivate concentration, you need to be able to focus on the present moment and take stock of the mental clutter that has accumulated in your mind. Too often, thoughts can become so jumbled and scattered that we forget to truly focus on the present moment and savour it. Seneca wrote extensively on this concept, stressing the importance of assessing your thoughts to gain clarity and insight.

The act of assessing both mental clutter and clarity of thought helps us identify sources of distraction as well as productive ideas to help us stay focused on what is important. For example, if you feel overwhelmed by your current workload, actively evaluate your situation. Note the areas where you need to slow down or reassess your strategy, and then get rid of any unnecessary clutter such as negative self-talk or irrational expectations. Knowing how to better manage our thoughts by actively monitoring them for irrationality allows us to take control over inner dialogue instead of becoming overwhelmed by negative self-talk or expectations.

Practicing mindfulness through meditation and other similar methods helps to promote clear thinking and peaceful contemplation. Such contemplative moments are precious. Reflective moments provide important insights from learning – all while sitting in contemplation, without using energy, or allowing yourself to become distracted. Taking time out each day for inner reflection keeps you mindful of your current state, so you can allocate energy more productively throughout life toward cultivating sustainable habits. In this way, you can also deal with problems that need to be resolved, instead of letting them build up over time and weighing you down. Dealing with such issues will free your mind to concentrate your efforts toward your meaningful goals, and your productivity will be increased through improved focus.

Through questioning what we think and how we think it, we are better able to make decisions grounded in reason rather than impulse. Over time, this practice will lead to an increased ability to stay calm during moments of stress, allowing you to utilise the power of presence more easily, which provides true depth and meaning in life's experiences. Consequently, cultivating concentration allows us to achieve more meaningful results with less effort, while also maintaining good mental health.

In conclusion, learning to assess the thoughts in your mind will help you to manage the clutter or noise that distracts from those that are meaningful. This skill will allow you to reflect and then manage problems that are distracting you from your meaningful goals. Mindfulness practices help you to clear your thoughts, find calm, and be present. Together, these skills will help you to be present in the moment, keep calm, and find the true depth and meaning in each of life's experiences.

Mindfulness and Directed Attention

Seneca understood that the world demands a great deal from us. Its complexity and multifaceted nature often overwhelms us and leaves us feeling distracted and unable to focus. Consequently, it's essential that we learn how to best use our attention to make the most of life's opportunities.

He maintained that distraction can be managed by actively recognising when we are becoming overwhelmed and allowing ourselves the time to become centred again. He believed that to achieve true clarity and peace of mind, we need to set aside moments of deliberation and actively cultivate mindfulness or "the power of attention" as he called it, enabling us to better tune into our innermost thoughts, rather than being swallowed up by external stimuli.

Other great thinkers echoed the importance of this concept: Socrates, "Beware the barrenness of a busy life"; James, "The faculty of voluntarily bringing back a wandering attention... is the very kernel of willpower";

and more recently, Tolle, "When you become aware of silence, immediately there is that state of inner still alertness."

Understanding our limited capacity for attention serves to help us cultivate concentration and lead more meaningful lives. No matter how frantic life may become at times, taking regular pauses allows us to better access our creative potential and overcome the inevitable mental clutter that builds up. It takes a pause to fully appreciate the power of that pause.

Seneca warned against allowing distraction to dominate our time. Attention is a limited resource which should be managed carefully to achieve meaningful results. Buddhist philosopher Thich Nhat Hanh explained, *"When you plant lettuce, if it does not grow well, you don't blame the lettuce. You look for reasons it is not doing well."* In other words, if we are frustrated with ourselves or lack fulfilment in our lives, it could be due to an inefficient use of our attention. This requires self-reflection and an active examination of what holds us back from being in the present moment.

Attention management is about more than just task prioritisation. It's about being mindful of how we spend our energy each day, and using our finite resources in a way that will bring us closer to achieving true satisfaction. It involves understanding how best to focus on one thing at a time, and letting go of competing interests rather than trying to tackle multiple projects. Attention management enables us to avoid temptations such as distracting social media notifications or web surfing, while also enabling us to take part in creative pursuits such as writing or painting.

The power of attention not only enables us to think more clearly, but also helps shape our values over time. We can train ourselves out of indulgent habits by redirecting energy toward productive activities that make use of our skills and capabilities.

In short, attention needs to be managed to avoid distractions, and this means pausing and taking time to do so. If you are not progressing in life, it may be because you are not allowing enough pause to manage your own internal dialogue and thoughts. Attention management allows distractions to be eliminated and focus to be fine-tuned to one thing at a time.

Self-Discipline and Purpose

In this modern age, it's easy to forget that our happiness does not come from material possessions or fleeting pleasures. True joy lies in the daily practice of living with intention, clarity, and fortitude. *"The greatest way to secure self-satisfaction is to live with purpose and discipline."* Seneca wrote extensively on this notion. He understood that life is too short to be spent aimlessly or haphazardly without valuing the hard work that goes into leading a meaningful existence. Seneca believed that happiness could be attained by understanding how best to use your time – whether this means taking part in meaningful activities or actively practicing mindfulness – thereby finding satisfaction through disciplined effort rather than aimless undirected existence.

Self-discipline is essential for developing good habits such as waking up early and setting achievable goals. By having a plan in place and following through on it, we can strive toward ever larger ambitions while also enjoying the satisfaction that comes with completing small tasks. Through progress with small tasks and being rewarded for each small success, you can begin to develop a sense of achievement and gratification as you follow your unique path in life.

Self-discipline is also key to discovering deep satisfaction in life because it allows us to take pride in our efforts by resisting distractions, maintaining composure during challenging situations, and avoiding short-term gratifications that only leave us empty in the long run. To become better versions of ourselves, self-awareness must be coupled with self-discipline. Once this equilibrium is reached, not only will our actions benefit us, they will also empower those around us.

Living with purpose means recognising what matters most to us, whether it's our relationships, our career aspirations, or simply being more mindful and present in each moment. Knowing our purpose means that we can direct our energy toward finding true fulfilment. It is only when we make conscious choices regarding how we spend our time, meaning time spent in alignment with our values and goals, that we can expect to experience true happiness and contentment. Although life has its hardships, if we remain steadfast in pursuing the things that bring us joy, then an underlying calm will pervade our daily lives.

Living with purpose requires setting boundaries and consistently following through on commitments. It means prioritising effort over outcome, and focusing on the present moment instead of trying to control the future. It requires adjusting your internal dialogue – constantly monitoring thoughts for irrationality – and proactively setting achievable objectives which are in line with greater but realistic ambitions.

By combining these two aspects of living – self-discipline and purpose – you can experience all of life's possibilities without becoming overwhelmed by them or sacrificing your inner peace. You will find deep satisfaction through self-discipline and living with intent. This approach will provide you with meaningful direction amidst the chaos of life.

Illusion of Eternity

Pablo Picasso once said, *"Only put off until tomorrow what you are willing to die having left undone."* You see, if we procrastinate or delay pursuing our ambitions, or wait too long before making a change for fear of failure, we may not be able to experience contentment later. Benjamin Franklin echoed this sentiment when he said, *"Do not squander time for that is the stuff life is made of."* (Poor Richard's Almanac, 1746). When faced with difficult decisions or seemingly unlimited possibilities, remember the importance of taking action now rather than deferring important goals until some undefined future point in time.

Seneca reminded us that we should not be deceived by life's illusory eternity and recognise instead that our own time is fleeting. Mary Oliver, the famous poet, advised, *"The world offers itself to your imagination, calls to you like the wild geese, harsh, and exciting – over and over announcing your place in the family of things."* With these words, she attempts to convey the sense of urgency that life requires. To actively embrace your mortality and prioritise meaningful moments, you must develop a sense of urgency. This entails understanding how best to utilise your energy throughout the day to ensure progress towards desired outcomes at work, in relationships, and even with respect to self-care.

Life is short and should never be taken for granted: it is important to make conscious decisions regarding how best to use our energy each day to avoid regret in the future. This means prioritising meaningful activities over trivialities; it means having firm boundaries that cannot be crossed without significant effort; and it also means understanding that there are no guarantees when it comes to success or happiness – only possibility with consistent effort.

Recognising that nothing lasts forever can help in terms of putting pursuits into perspective and providing clarity when difficult decisions need to be made. Don't take life for granted. Acknowledge that life is short rather than eternal, embrace mortality, and prioritise meaningful moments.

Prioritising

Seneca believed that time was the most precious commodity and should be managed carefully: *"We are not given a short life, but we make it short."* To this end, he championed the idea of actively managing our time to prioritise what matters and avoid wasting energy on activities that lack meaning.

Time management is not just about scheduling tasks or attempting to optimise efficiency, it is primarily an exercise in maintaining focus, self-discipline, and letting go of competing interests. Focusing on too many things simultaneously is an inefficient use of the precious resource of time, or as an ancient Chinese proverb teaches, *"If you chase two rabbits, you will lose them both."*

Time management involves spending energy wisely. We must think critically about what will bring us closer to achieving desired outcomes and which indulgent activities will reduce our productivity. If we are mindful of how we spend each day, time management can be used as a powerful tool for achieving our ambitions and making the most of life. Knowing when to focus on specific goals and prioritise essential tasks becomes particularly important when faced with an abundance of possibilities or distractions. As Warren Buffet once said, *"The difference between successful people and really successful people is that really successful people say no to almost everything."*

There is, however, no single formula for success. Each person has their own needs and limitations when it comes to managing their time, so what works for one person might not be feasible for another. Understanding how best to utilise resources available to achieve goals takes practice and dedication. Confucius advised:

"It does not matter how slowly you go as long as you do not stop." Strive for progress rather than perfection, and understand that small incremental steps will eventually lead you toward achieving meaningful goals over time.

Be honest with yourself regarding your capabilities. Being aware of our limitations can bring greater clarity in terms of what matters most. Also, understanding when to take breaks or delegate more complex projects enables us to focus on simpler tasks that add value while conserving energy for urgent endeavours such as job applications or studying for exams.

Equally important is using any extra time available – after meeting basic obligations – for creative pursuits. This could include experimenting with new hobbies, writing down ideas for later development, or networking with professionals in related fields. These are activities that not only bring joy, they also benefit other areas of life.

In short, prioritising time management is a discipline that shouldn't be taken lightly. It calls for taking control over the choices you make and ensuring effective use of resources without compromising your quality of life.

What's Essential?

Seneca states that our actions should be guided by a sense of purpose, not driven by the desire to accumulate material goods or prove ourselves for the sake of others. This is especially important when it comes to dealing with daily tasks and habits. Although some are essential for maintaining our physical and mental wellbeing, others can be removed without any detriment to our work or relationships.

Time spent on unnecessary tasks is time wasted. Instead of focusing on activities that take time away from our more meaningful pursuits, we should start eliminating them one by one to free up extra hours. Those hours can then be used to focus on what truly matters most. The elimination process could include minimising social media distractions or cutting out non-essential commitments. These may provide momentary pleasure, but they do little to improve our lives in the long run.

The same applies to habits that may have become routine over time. While these might appear harmless at first glance, forming too many unhealthy associations with certain activities can lead us astray further down the line if left unchecked. Lao Tzu once said, *"Simplicity, patience, compassion. These three are your greatest treasures."* Understanding how best to manage these components of life allows us to trim away anything superfluous and focus solely on what needs attention now.

Seneca believed that breaking away from society's expectations was essential for achieving true inner peace and satisfaction. By shedding unnecessary tasks and habits, we can ensure that each present moment is enjoyed for whatever it brings rather than constantly looking forward toward a distant idealised future. When faced with difficult decisions or seemingly limitless possibilities, it becomes particularly important to remember this philosophy, and to prioritise what matters most without becoming overwhelmed by competing interests and obligations.

Seneca teaches us that to make the most of our lives, we must remain aware of how and where we invest our time and effort. He believed that this kind of self-awareness was necessary for discerning what is truly essential from unnecessary distractions. This knowledge will help to free us up to act on our true priorities and avoid expending energy on activities that yield little or no benefit. We must learn to rid ourselves of commitments that produce minimal meaningful outcomes when our time could be better used for something else. Marcus was not present in the moment at his friend's wedding, tempted instead by the short-term attraction of seeing what his friends were up to on Instagram. Being able to discern the difference between spending time browsing social media and taking action toward his personal goal of meeting someone to have a meaningful relationship with will help him to abandon other time-wasting distractions in the future, consciously acting intentionally instead.

In addition, understanding how best to stay motivated during challenging periods can help boost productivity levels while avoiding burnout. Prioritising rest over perfectionism brings an element of balance into everyday life, allowing room for creativity and innovation. It is also beneficial to take breaks between intense sessions, allowing mind and body the chance to recover, or shift attention toward other tasks so as not to become overwhelmed by excessive demands – a notion reiterated by Thomas Edison in his famous quote, *"Restlessness and impatience are only incentives for greater exertion."*

Ultimately, Seneca cautions against wasting life in pointless endeavours. Instead, he urges us to make mindful decisions leading toward meaningful outcomes. Doing so means ridding ourselves of unnecessary activities that prevent us from reaching fulfilment. We need to understand that each moment counts and make appropriate choices accordingly.

Strategies to Stay Focused

Seneca advises that we should remain aware of where we direct our attention and energy throughout the day. Focus is a finite resource, often threatened by distractions or procrastination. This is particularly pertinent in modern times where technology, social media, and other sources of entertainment are designed to engage us. This can lead to balance being lost between essential and non-essential tasks. For this reason, it is important to create effective strategies for managing distractions that involve recognising individual needs and making conscious decisions based on them. In relation to focus, Steve Jobs once commented, *"People think focus means saying yes to the thing you've got to focus on. But that's not what it means at all... it means saying no to the hundred other good ideas that there are."*

The first step toward staying focused is to assess how much time is being spent on distracting activities. Tracking time over a period of days or weeks can paint an accurate picture of patterns in behaviour and provide insights into any issues requiring further attention or change. Once we have established this baseline, it should be used as a reference point against which future activities are measured. Further, identifying key moments when challenges arise (phone interruptions or friends calling round) allows us to tailor specific strategies to help combat them.

Seneca reminds us that our lives are too brief for meaningless pursuits. Instead, he urges us toward mastery over our thoughts and decisions so they may benefit both ourselves and those around us. Understanding our limitations and finding positive methods of controlling distractions enables us to stay focused on what matters most, forging ahead toward meaningful outcomes that will bring true fulfilment in life.

He suggests that to achieve our goals and make the most of life, we must stay focused on our ambitions despite the numerous distractions that exist to tempt us. In today's world, such distractions include technology, social media, and other forms of entertainment. Knowing when to use technology as a tool instead of letting it become the main focus helps ensure that distractions don't take over. The process of turning away from such temptations involves reinforcing positive behaviours over inefficient procrastination. This may include rewarding ourselves for completing difficult tasks, or regular check-ins with an accountability partner who can provide support during challenging periods.

One strategy to retain focus is to take breaks, working in short bursts of productivity instead of working for extended periods. Henry Ford once said, *"Nothing is particularly hard if you divide it into small jobs."* Breaking down major objectives into smaller chunks helps to keep momentum going while also reducing stress levels associated with tackling complex projects.

Using breaks between intense work sessions for creative pursuits is equally beneficial. Activities such as experimenting with new hobbies or networking with professionals in related fields allow time for refreshing the mind while providing additional perspective and energy to re-engage more effectively upon returning to a main task. Furthermore, being aware of our limitations can offer greater clarity regarding what matters most, and understanding when rest or delegation may be appropriate enables us to remain focused without compromising our quality of life.

Staying focused on what's essential requires courage alongside awareness. By carefully considering how and where we invest our energy each day, we can turn away from trivial pursuits while capitalising on opportunities that will ultimately help us reach our desired outcomes – living a fulfilled life free from distraction.

Lessons from Living in the Moment

If you are not progressing in life, it may be because you are not allowing enough pause to manage your own internal dialogue and thoughts. Attention management allows distractions to be eliminated and focus to be fine-tuned to one thing at a time.

Acknowledge the brevity of life, and take control over mindless, time-consuming distractions. Learn to distinguish between the activities that contribute to your meaningful goals and those that distract you from them, then direct your time and efforts toward meaningful occupations that enrich your life.

Identify the distractions or patterns of behaviour or thought that are not aligned with your personal ambitions, and refocus on your ultimate purpose in life.

Focus on now, rather than dwelling on regrets of the past or worries of the future. Accept life's events are sometimes out of your control; there is always something to be learned, and something to be grateful for in every eventuality and every day of our lives.

Learn to assess the thoughts in your mind, and to manage the clutter or noise distracting you from meaningful thoughts. Mindfulness practices will help you to be present in the moment, to stay calm, and to find true depth and meaning in life's experiences.

Identify how much time you are spending on distractions; make conscious decisions to refocus on your meaningful goals; stay focused with mastery over your thoughts, but take breaks, rest, and be prepared to delegate.

Time management is a discipline that shouldn't be taken lightly; it calls for taking control over your choices and ensuring effective use of resources. You will find deep satisfaction through self-discipline and living with intent. This approach will provide you with meaningful direction amidst the chaos of life.

Above all, don't take life for granted. Life is short, not eternal. Embrace mortality and prioritise meaningful moments.

Chapter 3

A Meaningful Life

Lily had been living in a state of constant stress for far too long. She was working full time, supporting her disabled mum, and often had to work overtime and night shifts. She rarely saw friends or socialised, had no time for check-ups at the dentist, or to have her hair cut. She felt like she was living life on the run, always sprinting to reach her next goal, and never giving herself the chance to savour the moment or appreciate what was really important.

It wasn't until she reached the point of total physical and emotional exhaustion that she realised she needed to think differently about the way she was living her life. One evening, although feeling unwell, she was on her way to cover a night shift, only to collapse as she got out of her car. A passer-by came to her aid, and then her manager drove her home. With a temperature of 39 degrees, she had to phone her aunt to ask her to help with her mum before taking to her bed. Her aunt took over the caring duties, including shopping and cooking, and this gave Lily a chance to recover. While she was in bed recovering, she had time to reflect on her life. Shocked by how much weight she had lost and how ill she had become so quickly, she decided it was time to take control of her life and start making conscious choices about what she focused on and gave her energy to.

To find more balance and peace, Lily began setting aside time specifically for self-care. It didn't matter whether this was just five minutes of quiet reading before bedtime or a full afternoon exploring her favourite park, it was establishing a habit of giving herself time each day to refuel her emotional resilience.

This also meant she had to be more selective about which projects she could take on at work, and to say 'no' more often instead of overloading herself with things that weren't truly necessary or meaningful. Doing so opened up space for the things in life that actually mattered, including spending time chatting with her mum – rather than just rushing around doing chores for her – and delving into creative hobbies that nourished her soul.

As soon as she started to devote more attention to making the most of life by focusing on what really mattered to her, Lily began noticing real changes. She found joy in simple moments instead of chasing after exaggerated dreams. She began to feel more connected with others and became grounded in a sense of calm despite the uncertainties around her.

In fact, it seemed that it didn't matter how stressful things got or how much chaos surrounded her, Lily could always come back home – both literally and figuratively – to a place where peace resided.

Focus

"It is not that we have a short time to live, but that we waste a lot of it. Life is long enough, and a sufficiently generous amount has been given to us for the highest

achievements if it were all well invested." – Seneca, On the Shortness of Life, 49AD. The American author Henry David Thoreau described Seneca's concept from a different perspective when he said, *"It is not enough to be busy. So are the ants. The question is: What are we busy with?"* In other words, the true value of time lies in using it wisely and purposefully.

Seneca argued that we must "focus on what matters" if we are to make the most of life, stating that, *"Life is long, if you know how to use it."* The meaning in his words is that we all have the opportunity to focus on what is important and to lead a life of true meaning. The Greek philosopher Socrates articulated this idea slightly differently when he said, *"The unexamined life is not worth living."* These words were spoken during his trial for impiety and corrupting youth in 399BC. By examining your life and focusing your attention on what matters, you can rise above the mundane and tap into a greater sense of purpose and satisfaction.

One way to stay focused on what matters is to create daily routines and practice them consistently over time. Habits help you to stay on track, even when motivation flags. Instead of waiting for inspiration or motivation, tackling tasks regularly will produce results more effectively than sporadic bursts of productivity. Creating habits can be a great way to stay focused on what matters most. Developing routines such as getting up early, staying organised, and setting aside time for meditation or reading can help to keep you focused on what is important in life. As Lily's story shows, carving out specific times during the day when you spend 10-20 minutes doing something enjoyable or creative is also worth considering. This will give you a break from more taxing activities such as work or study, allowing for some well-earned respite throughout your day.

In today's fast-paced world, it can be particularly difficult to focus on what matters and make the most of limited hours because we are constantly bombarded with information and distractions. This can leave us feeling overwhelmed and reduce our productivity. However, to quote Goethe, *"Things which matter most should never be at the mercy of things which matter least."* It's important to take control of your focus whenever you find yourself distracted. A good way to avoid distractions is to remove them from your environment, be it noisy colleagues or unnecessary notifications on mobile phones and computers, anything that diverts your attention away from productive activities should be eliminated, if possible. It's also important that you take regular breaks from technology as it can be one of the biggest distractions. Allowing yourself some digital downtime will give you space away from notifications and emails, giving you more time to focus on yourself and the things that matter most in life.

We can also learn from modern thought leaders on this subject such as the American educator Stephen R. Covey. He emphasises, *"The key is not to prioritise what's on your schedule, but to schedule your priorities"* – from The 7 Habits of Highly Effective People, 1989. By being intentional, you can ensure that you allocate your time and energy to things that are truly meaningful.

Moreover, as another great thinker reminds us, *"If you don't prioritise your life, someone else will"* – Greg McKeown, Essentialism: The Disciplined Pursuit of Less, 2014. You need to take responsibility for your actions and proactively decide which activities or values will bring you closer to achieving your ultimate goals. To make sure that you're using your time wisely and focusing on what matters most to you, it's essential to create a plan and set achievable goals. This way you can ensure that you are spending your days on meaningful activities, rather than wasting them on minor tasks or meaningless pursuits.

Being mindful of how you think about things is a valuable tool when it comes to focusing on what matters. If your thoughts are stuck in negative cycles such as regretting past events or worrying about things that may never happen, then this precious energy that could be directed elsewhere is lost. Focus on understanding your emotions rather than ruminating over things that cannot be changed. In this way, you will avoid wasting energy on unhelpful thoughts.

Take control of how you use your time and energy. Prioritise what matters, plan and schedule, create regular habits and routines, take breaks from technology, and keep a mindful approach. In so doing, you will be able to focus your attention on the important things, resulting in an overall improved quality of life.

Time's Value

Time is the most precious thing you have. You may surrender your money and property, but you cannot surrender time. Time is a commodity that we can never retrieve once it has elapsed, and everyone experiences time in their own way. It is something that motivates us to make a difference in our lives and can be used as an opportunity to live life to the fullest. The notion that our lives are fleeting has been echoed by many thinkers across time and space. The English poet William Shakespeare wrote, *"O! Be wise; what can you better spend than time?"* No matter how much we try, we cannot cheat the laws of nature – time marches on irrespective of who we are or what we do. Life should not be wasted, therefore, with meaningless activities. Instead, we should strive to achieve great things in the short span of our existence.

The true value of time is often not realised until it's too late; many people spend their days stressing about petty matters or planning for tomorrow rather than enjoying the present moment. While it's important to plan for the future, it's also important not to let those plans consume your life, leading to missing out on moments that should be filled with joy or contemplation. In the words of writer, religious thinker, and influential Quaker William Penn, *"Time is what we want most but what we use worst."*

Ultimately, time is a resource that needs to be handled carefully. When used properly, it can open up new opportunities or provide clarity on life's issues. When mismanaged, it may lead you down a path of regret. Benjamin Franklin advised, *"Do not squander time; for that's the stuff life is made of."* By being mindful of how we use our minutes and moments in life, we can maximise the output so that each day brings us closer to our goals and aspirations.

Time management plays an important role here. If you know how much time you have available each day, then you can structure your activities in a meaningful way that allows you to maximise your potential and make progress toward achieving goals or objectives faster than ever before. You will also gain more control over your emotions due to a better understanding of your limitations, helping to reduce stress levels and increase overall wellbeing.

Moreover, remember that time passes irrespective of whether anything is achieved during its course. What matters most is paying attention to its passing to ensure nothing important gets neglected or goes unexplored. As the American novelist Nathaniel Hawthorne said, *"Happiness is a butterfly which when pursued is just beyond your grasp, but if you sit down quietly may alight upon you."* This simple phrase offers insight into how our lives might look if we are truly utilising time's precious gift by focusing our efforts on what really matters at any given moment, rather than chasing after something out of reach. When Lily sat quietly to contemplate her life, she found peace.

Time is precious. Appreciate that life is fleeting, manage your time for activities which are meaningful, and avoid squandering time. Focus on what needs your attention right now, while still keeping your end goals in mind. Allow time to contemplate on life mindfully and in this way you will find peace.

Desires and Passions

What is the fruit of all our desires and passions if not to enjoy life? Understand yourself and your motivations, and in turn you will learn to manage your desires and passions to lead a fulfilling life. In his 2005 Stanford University address, Steve Jobs said, *"The only way to do great work is to love what you do."* What he meant us to understand from this is that striving for success becomes easier when we are passionate about it – whatever it is we are doing.

Knowing your own individual passion in life is essential. Robert Louis Stevenson emphasised this when he said, *"To know what you prefer instead of humbly saying 'Amen' to what the world tells you ought to prefer is to have kept your soul alive."* In other words, while it's important to take into account societal standards and expectations, it's equally important not to let them consume you entirely. Your passions are meant to empower you with joy, rather than enslave you into unhappiness. Understanding your own desires can also help you distinguish between things that offer only temporary satisfaction and those that bring lasting fulfilment.

The ancients believed that inner peace was achieved through moderation, often referred to as the 'golden mean.' Avoid extremes: don't overindulge, but don't deny either. Aristotle wrote, *"The extreme of pleasure is accompanied by pain; the extreme of pain is attended with danger. Only in the middle state, which may be called temperance, do men find safety."* This means seeking a balance between satisfying your wants and avoiding excesses forms an important part of leading a healthy lifestyle and mastering your emotions.

According to Seneca, *"The power of enduring labour conquers all things."* This is a powerful reminder that when it comes to managing your desires and passions in life, it is ultimately your discipline and perseverance that will determine your success. In the words of the American novelist, journalist, and activist Jack London, *"You can't wait for inspiration. You must go after it with a club."* Merely waiting around for something you want isn't enough, you must actively work toward it every day if you expect to get results.

However, the truth is that we often overestimate what we can achieve in a certain amount of time. You need to be aware of your own capabilities and limitations; this is essential when approaching tasks with passion and enthusiasm. Socrates challenged, *"Know thyself."* If we pause long enough to consider who we are, as well as what skills or flaws might be hindering us from achieving our goals, then we can finally begin to make progress toward realising whatever dreams or objectives we may have. As poet Rainer Maria Rilke noted, *"People have such a great capacity for doing what they want if only they really wanted it for long enough."* In other words, if you truly want something, then patience, discipline, and dedication are required to realise those aspirations.

This doesn't mean to imply that you should deny yourself pleasure or forget hedonistic pursuits altogether. On the contrary, an important aspect of any well-lived life involves enjoying yourself and having moments of leisure with family and friends. Lao Tzu recommended, *"A way to do is to be."* To this end, it may be best to think about the management of your passions as a balancing act between allowing yourself moments of indulgence while also exercising restraint and being mindful of how productive you are over the course of any given day.

Managing your passions requires balancing extremes. Indulging without overindulging; recognising societal standards but still following your own dreams; seeking inspiration and actively working toward your aspirations, all while accepting that having too much or too little isn't beneficial either way. By proactively managing these opposing forces – forces that are at play in everyone's lives – you can successfully attain greater goals while still finding joy in everyday moments along the way.

Self-Discipline

According to Seneca, *"He who learns must suffer. And even in our sleep, pain that cannot forget falls drop by drop upon the heart and in our own despair, against our wills, comes wisdom to us by the awful grace of God."* This speaks volumes about the importance of self-discipline in life. If you hope to achieve success or mastery over a particular task then you must be willing to make sacrifices and work hard, even during times when it may not be convenient.

The notion of the need to endure hardship to succeed has been echoed by many other thinkers across time and space. British prime minister Winston Churchill once famously said, *"Success is not final; failure is not fatal. It is the courage to continue that counts."* Whatever goals you have, they must always be accompanied by an internal drive to develop habits that enable you to reach them.

Given how quickly technology has advanced, it can appear that shortcuts to everything are available at every turn, but this often tempts us away from learning important skills such as critical thinking and problem-solving. These are skills that can only truly take shape through educational processes such as trial-and-error or trial-by-fire experiences. For sustainable progress to occur, we must set aside moments for personal growth wherever possible, whether it is taking time out here and there to read a book, or taking on a side project with friends, providing an opportunity for everyone involved to stretch their skillsets in unexpected ways.

Ultimately, self-discipline involves pushing yourself outside of your comfort zone to gain wider perspectives on what might be achievable with enough dedication and hard work. It is about recognising that immediate gratification is temporary, and delayed gratification may reflect true success. As the American author Jim Rohn said, *"Discipline is the bridge between goals and accomplishments."* Recognising the power of discipline within yourself can truly unlock massive potential, and self-discipline is an important component of the unlocking process. It helps us focus on getting the tasks at hand done with efficiency and accuracy, rather than succumbing to procrastination or other negative habits that may hinder our productivity. Einstein wrote,

"It's not that I'm so smart; it's just that I stay with problems longer."

Self-discipline also helps us make decisions that may not always be to our immediate liking but will be beneficial in the long term. An example of this could be choosing activities that foster creativity or health rather than indulging in idle distractions such as scrolling through social media mindlessly for hours on end. Taking responsibility for your actions requires a certain degree of willingness to accept the discomfort of maintaining the necessary focus and drive to achieve desired outcomes. There is an African proverb which reads, *"When there is no enemy within, the enemies outside can do you no harm."*

Staying motivated to keep moving toward your goals is another key element of achieving meaningful results in whatever field you might pursue. As the American entrepreneur Jim Rohn voices, *"Motivation is what gets you started; habit is what keeps you going."* To this end, developing healthy routines such as exercising regularly or reading inspirational books can be helpful tools in terms of keeping you on track, but allowing moments of relaxation every now and then should also be part of any successful discipline-building routine.

It is self-discipline that allows you to take control over how you use your limited resources – particularly time – allowing you to maximise its benefit in terms of achieving your dreams. Having internal drive, supporting your personal growth, maintaining your motivation with healthy routines, practicing self-discipline with perseverance, and avoiding indulgences will all help you achieve a productive and accomplished life.

Success

Seneca said, *"If one does not know to which port one is sailing, no wind is favourable."* His words remind us that when it comes to pursuing success and personal fulfilment in life, it is essential to have a clear idea of exactly what that means to you.

We can be inundated with messages through society or media that attempt to define success by means of wealth or power. This narrow view won't necessarily bring us true contentment in the long run. As expressed by Confucius, *"Choose a job you love, and you will never have to work a day in your life."* Rather than fixating on external recognition for your achievements or career status, it's important to cultivate a sense of purpose within yourself to ensure your efforts throughout the journey remain meaningful. Seneca famously noted, *"It is quality rather than quantity that matters."* This message in this maxim is that success and personal fulfilment should not be measured by external standards such as wealth or fame, but by your own individual achievements.

In the words of naturalist, essayist, poet, and philosopher Henry David Thoreau, *"Rather than love, than money, than fame; give me truth."* This idea of finding happiness through internal validation is an important reminder that what truly matters in life is your own opinion of any particular situation, not the opinions of others or society at large. For this purpose, it helps to engage regularly in self-reflection to gain better insight into how you are feeling about your current path, and whether it aligns with what will bring you true purpose and fulfilment.

At the same time, it's valuable to remind yourself that there are still ebbs and flows during any goal-oriented process. These ups and downs should be accepted as part of life's inevitable difficulties alongside opportunities to celebrate when accomplishments are reached. As journalist Elbert Hubbard once said, *"The line between failure and success is so fine that we scarcely know when we pass it – so fine that we often are on the line and do not know it."* Success isn't defined solely by reaching a desired endpoint, it can also be based on the effort put in to achieving each target along the way. Success and personal fulfilment requires a balancing act between a willingness to confront challenges head on and giving yourself room for rest and relaxation. When this balance is achieved, you have what you need to remain focused on objectives over any period of time without becoming drained by them.

Only you know why certain goals are important to you, and using this awareness to craft an approach uniquely tuned for your specific lifestyle can prove invaluable in leading a happy life full of meaning. Ultimately, finding a balance between aiming for ambitious goals *and* enjoying everyday moments can be immensely satisfying for those who recognise their unique gifts and determine their own definitions of achievement. In this way, no wind will seem unfavourable nor too challenging. Joy from reaching destination points along the voyage become aspects worthy of celebration throughout your journey toward discovering true fulfilment in life.

Finances

"No one is more wretched than someone who delights in riches only." Variations of this statement have been spoken by numerous thinkers over the centuries, and it serves to highlight the importance of living within your means if you are to truly enjoy the gifts life offers us – both material and emotional. Living within your means is simply ensuring your daily expenditures do not exceed your resources, thereby avoiding getting into debt or other financial trouble.

Living within your means can be achieved through smart financial planning for both short- and long-term objectives, and by finding creative ways to increase revenue streams if needed over time. Budgeting helps keep track of expenses, and helps to prepare for unexpected costs that may arise such as accidents or sudden medical bills. As noted by American investor Warren Buffett, *"Do not save what is left after spending but spend what is left after saving."* Such accounting strategies are healthy habits for managing personal finances. You should remain in control of your destiny by investing any extra money you have into savings and other investments, rather than spending it on frivolous items or activities that won't bring you any closer to your long-term goals. As well as helping to ensure financial stability for you, this practice plays a major role in being able to lead a meaningful life with purpose and fulfilment.

Living within your means implies taking responsibility for understanding your personal budget and recognising where cuts in expenses may be made to ensure a more frugal lifestyle. Examples might be forgoing expensive meals out or trading certain material possessions for more rewarding experiences such as travel or outdoor activities. Living within your means can also mean limiting consumerism by only buying items essential to sustaining your lifestyle, therefore avoiding impulse purchases such as clothes in a sale when you don't need them. Choose instead to make reasoned decisions about purchases. As the American entrepreneur Jay Shetty pointed out, *"You don't need more stuff; you need time, space, clarity, stillness, less distractions, and fewer commitments."* With these words, Shetty emphasised that sometimes having less can allow you to enjoy life more.

Henry David Thoreau once said, *"Wealth is the ability to fully experience life."* True prosperity rests within your own values and sense of internal satisfaction, rather than in gathering excessive amounts of possessions or striving to maintain a false image of what success means. It allows you to cultivate a greater understanding of your needs and wants, while remaining content with whatever you may have at any particular moment.

Living within your means provides a sense of independence by giving you access to resources otherwise lost if poor financial decisions had been made. This allows you to craft a lifestyle specifically tailored toward your own individual goals without relying on external factors such as credit cards or loans. Embracing the principle of living within your means protects a future for you in which you are free of fear over access to short-term funds when needed.

In practice, it requires careful budgeting, monitoring of expenses, saving where you can, and limiting consumerism to live within your means. However, when this is achieved, you are able to live independently without fear of debt, or worries over raising emergency funds, and you are in a position to remain focused on your meaningful goals in life.

Careers, Hobbies, and Relationships

As noted by American businessman Jim Rohn, *"Successful people don't just work hard; they work smart."* Of course, striking a balance between numerous commitments can prove difficult at times, and it's something that requires a combination of discipline, self-awareness, and creativity.

Investing in professional development should remain a priority. This is where both planning and maximising available resources play important roles in helping you move ahead in your field without becoming drained from doing too much. The French writer Antoine de Saint-Exupéry wisely stated, *"A goal without a plan is just a wish."* Adopting strategies that provide insight into what needs to be done ahead of time helps alleviate stress when unexpected roadblocks appear along our paths, and allow us to remain flexible when dealing with the realities of modern life.

Investing in personal relationships helps promote better physical and mental health, giving a greater sense of belonging which boosts confidence. Improving connections through networking, or spending time nurturing existing bonds, will help you to create more sustainable frameworks for future personal growth. This, in turn, will help buffer any potential setbacks you encounter along the way. You will then move toward achieving professional prosperity alongside meaningful personal relationships.

English entrepreneur Richard Branson believes, *"You don't have to be connected all the time. What matters are the moments when you come together and create something great."* This idea further reinforces the importance of maintaining balance between various aspects of life, such as spending quality time with family or taking leisurely breaks from work to refocus energy for a return to more productive activities. Doing so helps us lead meaningful lives with purpose, while still adhering to whatever goals we may have set for ourselves professionally.

Engaging in hobbies regularly serves as an excellent outlet for creativity, especially when dealing with taxing situations caused by our professional obligations. Journalist Bill Bryson eloquently captured this idea when he said, *"We must all make time each day for recreation and rest if we are ever going to have true success."* Making time in this way allows you to not only refresh physically, but also mentally before tackling new endeavours. This can be of particular value in demanding jobs and during heavy workload periods.

When scheduling your day-to-day activities, allow yourself the important luxury of balance between professional work, professional development, building connections with others, and hobbies. All these facets of life contribute to physical and mental wellbeing, and therefore toward living a meaningful and fulfilled life.

Diet and Exercise

"A sound mind in a healthy body is the best of fortune." Seneca's words reflect the importance of taking care of yourself both physically and mentally to enjoy the gifts that life offers you, especially when entering the later stages in life. Maintaining health through proper diet and exercise should become part of your daily routine throughout life, thereby helping to prevent avoidable health conditions associated with poor lifestyle choices.

As noted by the American nutritionist Jonny Bowden, *"Healthy eating isn't about deprivation; it's all about making good choices so you can give your body the nutrition it needs and craves without going overboard."* Eating nutritious meals serves as an important foundation for building and maintaining good health, as well as fuelling day-to-day activities. Giving your body what it needs requires knowledge of the nutrients that are essential for proper development. A healthy balance of carbohydrates, proteins, fats, vitamins, and minerals is needed to help reduce fatigue, combat stress-related illnesses, boost energy levels, and keep your body running like a well-oiled machine. Don't let ignorance, carelessness, or just plain laziness lead to missing out on daily nutritional requirements; be mindful of what you consume on a regular basis.

Regular exercise also plays a vital role in keeping you fit both physically and mentally. This doesn't necessarily mean working out in gyms for extended periods, it can simply be whatever activity works best for you and fits in with your lifestyle. Cycling, swimming, and running are popular forms of physical activity, but there are many more ways to stay active and *enjoy* doing it, not least taking a daily walk in a local park or getting out for a ramble in the countryside. In short, getting and staying active needn't involve health club memberships, all it takes is finding an activity you enjoy doing, and then you'll be much more inclined to do it regularly as part of your lifestyle.

Making it a habit can be achieved by creating daily or weekly schedules that incorporate planned exercise activities alongside mandatory tasks. Developing routines that allow you to focus on what needs to get done with built-in exercise breaks can be a useful tool for managing stress in demanding jobs that may require long hours, but ultimately, being conscious of diet and exercise in everyday life is essential for living a healthy, productive life filled with purpose. This lifestyle will empower you mentally and physically, and support your personal growth.

Gratitude

"Gratitude is not only the greatest of virtues, but the parent of all others." These wise words spoken by Seneca demonstrate his fundamental belief that we should acknowledge and appreciate everything life has to offer. All things, from simple pleasures such as happy times spent with family and friends to bigger happenings such as promotions at work, or any other complex achievement, are things to be grateful for.

Through being thankful and appreciating what comes our way every day, no matter how big or small, we remain open to experiences that are greater than ourselves. American painter and writer Henry Miller once said, *"The moment one gives close attention to anything, even a blade of grass, it becomes a mysterious, awesome, indescribably magnificent world in itself."* These words encourage us to remain mindful when engaged in any task so we can appreciate the beauty within each present moment.

Blaise Pascal noted, *"All men's miseries derive from not being able to sit in a quiet room alone."* Herein lies a simple truth that offers much food for thought: it is easier to cultivate gratefulness by bringing your attention within, rather than always looking outwards, chasing material gain or pleasure-seeking activities. Solitude provides an environment in which to deeply contemplate all there is to be truly thankful for without distractions getting in the way. Cultivating gratitude for all we have requires a degree of effort and spiritual awareness mixed with practical application, but once earnestly established, this easy habit will bring immense benefits in terms of letting go of mental stress and allowing space to create new pathways to understanding the joy life brings us on a daily basis.

Rumi reminds us, *"Yesterday I was clever, so I wanted to change the world. Today I am wise, so I am changing myself."* Here lies an even deeper truth: appreciating what you have also means being comfortable with who you are and valuing your own worth above anything else. This requires patience and humility. It takes time to truly come into alignment with yourself, and to find peace in your own life before looking outwardly at others or your environment.

The timeless words of wisdom from some of humanity's greatest thinkers highlight the importance of cultivating gratitude for the world around us. Through gratitude, you can appreciate something in every moment, and through internal reflection, you can learn to appreciate yourself. Only through developing an attitude of appreciative awareness can true fulfilment be attained.

Meaningful Connections

The key to creating meaningful connections with those around you lies in understanding the power of community. The views of other thought leaders on this topic further illustrate this fact. Martin Luther King Jr. said, *"We may have all come on different ships, but we're in the same boat now."* This statement reminds us of the importance of looking beyond our backgrounds and embracing humanity as one people. Gandhi also recognised the value of building relationships and fostering community when he said, *"You must be the change you wish to see in the world."* This was a call for collective action, encouraging individuals to act inclusively and compassionately toward their neighbours.

Making meaningful connections with others means investing time in yourself and your own personal growth. This begins by listening closely to your inner voice and creating meaningful relationships from within. It's about being yourself as your best self, or as

Ralph Waldo Emerson put it, "What you do speaks so loudly that I cannot hear what you say." By understanding the power of community, recognising your shared humanity, being mindful of your actions, and tuning into yourself, you can create meaningful bonds with those around you; bonds that will last longer than any material thing or fleeting moment in life.

In the age of technology and social media, we have become increasingly isolated from one another despite having instant access to more people than ever before. The only way to break this disconnect and the loneliness and anxiety it creates is to foster a sense of community, belonging, and purpose.

One of the most effective ways to build genuine connections with others is to simply listen. When we engage in active listening – meaning that we allow others to fully express their thoughts and feelings without interrupting or passing judgment – we create an environment in which both parties feel heard and understood. Active listening also allows for greater levels of trust and empathy between parties, and this helps to strengthen the connection between them.

Albert Schweitzer once stated, *"The only ones among you who will be really happy are those who will have sought and found how to serve."* By focusing on serving other people instead of yourself, you can create mutual relationships where both parties benefit from giving and receiving emotional support. By prioritising these selfless acts of kindness toward others, you will forge deeper bonds that can outlast even physical distance or time spent apart.

ROBERT N. JACOBS

When creating meaningful connections with others, it's important to remember Jim Rohn's wise words. He said, *"You are the average of the five people you spend the most time with."* Ensure that the people you choose to surround yourself with add value to your life rather than detract from it. Those who inspire you, challenge you mentally and emotionally, teach you new things about life, and offer encouragement during difficult times will help you grow. Those who offer criticism or pessimism instead of support will block you.

It may not always be easy in today's world, but building true connections has never been more important for your personal wellbeing, or for the collective health of society. Being surrounded by family members or long-term friends can sometimes make you forget, or take for granted, just how valuable those genuine relationships are. Taking action today to begin forming meaningful connections with others could drastically improve life not only for you, but for others too. You can achieve this by recognising the value of community, tuning in to yourself, practicing active listening, and acting kindly towards others. Remember that to improve yourself, you also need to choose your friends carefully. If you surround yourself with kind, engaged friends, you will become one yourself.

Lessons from a Meaningful Life

Take control of how you use your time and energy by prioritising what matters, planning, scheduling, creating regular habits and routines, taking breaks from technology, and keeping a mindful approach.

Appreciate that time is precious and life is fleeting. Manage your time for activities that are meaningful, while also allowing time to contemplate on life mindfully.

Managing your passions requires a balance of extremes: indulge without overindulging, and recognise societal standards while still following your own dreams.

Practice self-discipline to persevere, sustain your internal drive and motivation to maintain healthy routines, support your personal growth, and avoid indulgences.

Determine your own definitions of achievement, and use this to craft your own unique approach to leading a life of purpose, meaning, and fulfilment.

To live within your means, budget carefully, monitor expenses, save where you can, and limit consumerism.

When scheduling your day-to-day activities, give yourself the important luxury of maintaining balance between work, professional development, building connections with others, and hobbies.

Remain conscious of your diet and exercise habits for healthy living.

Be grateful for all things. Through gratitude, you can appreciate something in every moment, and through internal reflection, you can learn to appreciate yourself.

Build connections with people by recognising the value of community, tuning in to yourself, practicing active listening, acting kindly towards others, and choosing your friends carefully.

Chapter 4

Seizing Opportunities

Growing up in India, Ajeet was surrounded by people who taught him the importance of hard work and perseverance, both essential traits to succeed in life. He studied and passed his exams; he went to university and studied some more. When he was qualified, he was offered several jobs in banks, all close to his family. He met a beautiful young woman and married her, and they had two wonderful children. After a few years, he fell into a routine with his family and children, and noticed that life was comfortable and safe. His wife was happy and told him he shouldn't worry; life was good, and they could relax and enjoy themselves. For a while, he became complacent.

One day, Ajeet was watching his children play in the garden and reflecting on his working life. He had been working at the bank for five years and knew how to do everything that was needed there. He didn't need more money or the kudos of promotion, but he felt unfulfilled. He felt something was missing. As he reflected on his situation, he realised that he wasn't growing. He had seen many young trainees join the bank, and watched them make mistakes and lose their confidence. It was easy for Ajeet to correct their work for them, but perhaps he should be doing more. Thinking about his own lack of personal growth, and the junior assistants' need for guidance and support, he decided to become their mentor. He spoke to his boss about this and followed a teaching course at night school. Instead of correcting the juniors' errors, he started to teach the junior staff how to learn from their mistakes.

Ajeet became the bank's trainer in addition to his own duties. He soon felt fulfilled as he watched his trainees grow and develop in confidence and skills. His reflections in the garden that day as he watched his children play had opened up a new opportunity for him. Soon he was teaching the more experienced juniors how to help the new recruits and looking for a new opportunity himself. Years later, Ajeet became a professor and taught at the university where he himself had studied.

Self-Reflection

Seneca warned that: *"We squander our lives in careless living when we make no effort at self-reflection."* He encouraged others to think deeply about their decisions and be aware of how they were influencing their lives. He believed that introspection to better understand yourself would help identify bad habits and how to improve them.

Self-reflection can be a key to unlocking personal growth and success. It involves taking some time out of everyday life to reflect on your own thoughts, emotions, actions, and experiences. Through this process, you can gain better insight into your life and understand the areas where improvement is needed. Self-reflection has many benefits: it can help us develop emotional intelligence, sharpen our problem-solving skills, encourage resilience in difficult times, reduce stress levels, increase mental clarity, and generally boost overall wellbeing.

Taking a step back to analyse your own behaviour is an important exercise that should be incorporated into your daily routine, allowing you to become more mindful and build upon your strengths to reach your full potential. Through reflection, Ajeet was able to acknowledge his complacency, and recognise an opportunity at his work that would help him grow as a person and develop his own skills. Self-reflection is an essential part of understanding yourself and uncovering areas for growth. The power lies within all of us to reflect and better understand who we really are, and recognise any areas for improvement. Action can then be taken for personal growth.

However, this requires courage. It's easy to shy away from introspection through fear of discovering something unpleasant about yourself. Although self-reflection may reveal uncomfortable facets of yourself, actively choosing not to address issues, or burying them rather than thinking about them, only serves as an obstacle in your journey toward personal growth. Without self-reflection, Ajeet would have remained complacent and would not have recognised the opportunity to develop his skills and grow as a person.

Reflection provides clarity, helping you to understand yourself better, and enabling you to uncover fresh perspectives on familiar problems or challenges that otherwise would have remained stagnated. In turn, this process enables you to make well-informed decisions, helping to propel you toward achieving your desired goals efficiently, and become the best version of yourself at every step along the way.

Courage and Confidence

Courage and boldness are essential qualities for seizing opportunities with confidence. Muhammad Ali once said, *"He who is not courageous enough to take risks will accomplish nothing in life."* Eleanor Roosevelt also aptly phrased this sentiment when she said, *"You gain strength, courage, and confidence by every experience in which you really stop to look fear in the face."* Overcoming fear empowers us to reach our goals more easily since we are no longer held back by apprehension.

The benefits of possessing this mindset are countless. Having courage helps us take risks without fear, no matter how daunting the risks may seem. Courage gives us freedom and autonomy. It's only when we push ourselves out of our comfort zone that we realise what is within our capability.

There's always a chance of failure, but by consistently striving to be courageous we become open to new possibilities, and we can learn from our mistakes while enjoying success along the way. As Winston Churchill once said, *"Success consists of going from failure to failure without loss of enthusiasm."* Fearlessness brings us closer to achieving greatness in everything we do on our journey toward self-discovery and growth. Moving out of your comfort zone is always frightening, but one step at a time is all it takes. Ajeet had to do it; he had to approach his managers with a new idea and risk losing his comfortable day-to-day routines.

Taking ownership means facing challenges bravely and taking decisive action when required. The American entrepreneur Biz Stone put this into words when he said, *"Be bold enough to use your voice, brave enough to listen to your heart, and strong enough to live the life you've always imagined."* Having this level of courage and confidence turns obstacles into experiences that help to shape your personality and hone your skillset, allowing you to seize whatever comes across your path with clarity and confidence.

Courage and boldness are essential for seizing opportunities with confidence. Courage can be seen as a prerequisite for success: without a willingness to take risks or make changes, there can be no hope of moving forward.

Embracing Change

It is the duty of every wise person to reflect on the changeableness of human life and adapt to it. Adapting to change may require us to let go of past experiences or beliefs as they no longer serve any purpose. The American author Wayne Dyer wrote: *"Change the way you look at things and the things you look at change."*

We must be willing to accept that we have outgrown certain aspects of our lives and move on with grace to progress in life. Ajeet changed the way he looked at his life. Instead of accepting the comfort of his routine and manageable life, he looked to see how he could use his time more effectively to grow and feel more fulfilled.

Embracing change provides us with more power and control over our own lives. It turns us away from old paths, allowing us to forge new paths that lead to improved versions of ourselves. While it may involve some initial discomfort during transition periods, this process will lead to a brighter future filled with better opportunities. Change can often bring about a new perspective, helping us explore different options that we wouldn't have seen before. It helps us break away from monotony and divert our energies toward something more meaningful and purposeful.

Change can be difficult at times because it pushes us outside our comfort zone, forcing us to face unforeseen challenges or experiences. However, change is a natural and necessary part of life. If we allow ourselves to embrace what comes our way with openness and enthusiasm, instead of resistance or cynicism, we will experience far greater levels of growth than if we turn away from change through fear or discomfort.

Change can only be embraced when we take ownership of our circumstances and look inward for improvement. Peter Drucker noted, *"Change is not made without involvement and commitment."* Taking personal responsibility for areas of growth gives us clarity that encourages us to welcome change instead of rejecting it.

Change allows us to act upon fresh perspectives and seize new opportunities. It can be seen as a catalyst for personal development. By being open to new possibilities we can emerge stronger than ever before. Change is inevitable, but embracing it brings growth. *"The whole future lies in uncertainty: live immediately."* – Seneca, On the Shortness of Life, 49AD.

Living Intentionally

Seneca emphasised the importance of understanding what truly matters, rather than living with a false sense of importance or urgency placed on everyday activities that do not contribute toward meaningful pursuits. *"...No human enterprise will come true until there has gone forth from your heart something which must have first come from your mind."*

Many modern thought leaders have added to this line of thinking. American entrepreneur Marie Forleo said, *"Successful living isn't about chasing after certain outcomes; it's about aligning your inner self with whatever it is that brings you joy."* Steve Jobs stated, *"Your time is limited, so don't waste it living someone else's life...have the courage to follow your heart and intuition."*

Living intentionally can be difficult. It requires planning, focus, and sometimes sacrifice, especially when surrounded by so many sources of distraction and busyness. It's easy to get distracted by external pressures and societal expectations, but if you take the time to reflect deeply on your purpose in life, your actions will naturally flow from there. By shifting away from frenetic activity and seeking moments where you can reflect deeply on what matters most, you can find a new resonance within yourself that provides long-term benefits throughout your life's journey, supporting you as you strive to achieve authentic success.

Once you have identified what values and pursuits are meaningful to you, ask yourself an important question when making decisions or setting goals: "Does this contribute to my overall wellbeing in a meaningful way?" This practice will help keep you focused on what really matters, and prevent unproductive pursuits from taking over your life.

By understanding your own desires and values, and staying true to them even when faced with adversity or temptation, you can make meaningful progress toward achieving authentic success.

Playing the Long Game

As modern society continues at its breakneck speed of change, we often struggle to find a balance between time spent in the present and time devoted to future plans. The key to striking this balance lies in finding ways to play the long game.

Life is a series of moments, and it can be easy to focus so much on the present that we forget about the future. We need to remember that long-term goals and successes are often just as important as our short-term ones, and we must find ways to embrace both the present moment and think toward the long term. In other words, play the long game while embracing moments now. Playing the long game while still appreciating every moment will set you up for lasting success and meaningfully enrich your life experience. Success is not always achieved through immediate gratification but through consistent dedication.

Creating balance between the immediate demands of life and longer-term aspirations requires us to prioritise our time according to what's most important. Emphasis should be placed on creating a foundation that will help you achieve success over a longer period of time, otherwise you run the risk of becoming trapped in an endless cycle of short-term accomplishments that ultimately do not lead anywhere.

Playing the long game means learning how to make small, incremental changes that can eventually lead to greater results. This can be achieved by taking small steps toward achieving your ultimate goal. Break down your goals into manageable parts, and then assign yourself achievable deadlines for each part to make steady progress without feeling overwhelmed. For example, if your long-term goal is to plan for a secure retirement, one of your short-term goals might include investing in retirement accounts. If your long-term goal is to be promoted, you may need to achieve some smaller steps to help you get there, such as training in a certain topic. As Jack Ma, founder of Alibaba Group, once pointed out, *"Today's pain is tomorrow's gain."* It also means learning to savour the moments of joy and peace amidst challenging circumstances – no matter how brief they may be – and using them as fuel for long-term goal setting and achievement. Ajeet took advantage of a time when demands were not high in his life, and he felt at peace to reflect and consider how he could plan for his future. Each day offers us opportunities to plan ahead while appreciating our lives now.

By completing smaller tasks today that contribute to your larger goal for the future, you will create your path toward success. Find ways to play the long game while embracing each moment life brings you now.

Thriving in Uncertainty and Adversity

It can be incredibly challenging to thrive in times of uncertainty and adversity. As Seneca said, *"Difficulties strengthen the mind, as labour does the body."* The author and motivational speaker Anthony Robbins has also said, *"It's not what happens that has the greatest power over us; it's how you interpret what happens and the action you take as a result of your interpretation."* When faced with hardships, it is essential to remain focused on what you can control. You can actively choose how to react in any situation beyond your control.

Victor Frankl famously voiced this belief when he said, *"Everything can be taken from a man but one thing: the last of human freedoms – to choose one's attitude in any given set of circumstances...to choose one's own way."* You must strive for this sense of inner control and determination amid times of turmoil if you wish to maintain equanimity in uncertain situations. By exercising this discipline, you can channel your energies into constructive activities that will help you emerge stronger than ever before. Uncertainty and adversity are natural components of life, but it is how we respond to these challenges that determines our success.

In moments of difficulty and ambiguity, it can be beneficial to seek guidance from those who have encountered similar obstacles in life, either through their own experiences or those they have observed. Taking others' experiences into consideration helps build resilience during trying times. Their success in overcoming such challenges suggests that if you persevere and stay optimistic about your future prospects, you will succeed too.

Uncertainty and adversity are not always negative. As the Dalai Lama said, *"Remember that not getting what you want is sometimes a wonderful stroke of luck."* What we think we need may be different from our destiny. Another way of looking at uncertainty and adversity is suggested by the famous poet Ranier Maria Rilke who wrote: *"Be patient toward all that is unsolved in your heart and try to love the questions themselves like locked rooms..."* Difficult moments can often be transformed into learning experiences, and your successes and failures are part of your journey toward growth.

Adversities may not always be negative, or if they are, others have overcome them and will be able to guide you through. Uncertainty and adversity are a part of life out with your control, but how you respond to them is within your control, so channel your energies wisely.

Embrace Failure

More than two thousand years ago, Seneca made the argument that failure should be embraced and by no means avoided: *"Let us practice failing well: let us fail with greatness."* His point is that we can never learn skilfully unless we acknowledge our failures at each step. Life will often challenge us, but we need to view these events with an open mind and use them as catalysts for growth. We need to learn from our mistakes, accept them, and move on. The same concept is essential for success today. Take risks and accept when something doesn't go according to plan; only then can you move on from failure and uncover new possibilities.

We will never reach excellence or attain greatness if we continue to let fear and anxiety keep us from exploring new opportunities. Often, those who take the biggest risks can reap the greatest rewards since they have the courage to venture into uncharted territory. To be successful, we must shift our thinking away from being afraid of failure and instead focus on what can be learned. It's essential to acknowledge our mistakes rather than allow them to discourage us. After all, there is no real failure if we learn something in the process.

As Albert Einstein argued, *"A person who never made a mistake never tried anything new."* By understanding that failure has its place in life, we gain access to paths that would otherwise remain hidden from us. We can view each mistake as an opportunity for growth and improvement, rather than an obstacle blocking our path. The Swiss philosopher Henri Frederic Amiel added to this line of thought when he said, *"No man succeeds without a good measure of courage, risk taking ability, and most importantly a strong belief in himself."* The key is having faith in ourselves even when things don't work out as planned – this enables us to eventually succeed where others give up or simply don't know how to begin.

Seneca's wisdom informs us that, *"It is not because things are difficult that we do not dare; it is because we do not dare that things are difficult."* Let go of fear-based thinking and embrace change with enthusiasm. Stop striving for 'perfect' results and start looking at every experience as valuable feedback that helps you develop further skills. Once you do this, you'll be able to open yourself up to more possibilities than ever before. Successful entrepreneur Richard Branson echoed similar sentiments when he said, *"If you look closely at those who have failed without giving up, they eventually push through their obstacles and achieve success."* He too stresses the importance of learning from failure instead of avoiding it altogether.

Don't be afraid of failure because it is the lessons learned that help propel you forward in life. Embrace failure as an opportunity to grow stronger and smarter. Be brave at taking risks and trying new things, fail well, and learn from your mistakes.

Incremental Growth

Seneca extolled the power of small steps and incremental growth in achieving great success. This power should not be underestimated as it leads us toward meaningful accomplishments that could never have been achieved without taking small, productive steps every day. Highly successful people understand this notion well and live by it, taking a step at a time until they arrive at their destination. It takes more than just courage to change, it takes persistence and determination.

Research supports this approach. Studies show that small improvements, when made regularly and consistently over time, create more enduring results than drastic changes or massive investments. Many thought leaders echo this thinking. Behavioural economist Dan Ariely once said, *"Small daily actions are far better predictors of success than any big event will be,"* and Albert Einstein famously noted, *"Life is like riding a bicycle. To keep your balance, you must keep moving."* Small steps, if taken consistently with focus and intention, can lead to big advances. In this way, seemingly insignificant actions can accumulate into tremendous power.

The power of incremental growth can be seen in many areas, not least business and education. Small investments made over time can lead to great gains. For instance, students who work consistently toward their degree will eventually see the fruits of their labour when they complete their studies. We can also apply this concept to our personal lives and relationships. By making small changes over time, we can create lasting friendships and meaningful connections with others. In all aspects of life, taking a slow and steady approach (rather than trying to find shortcuts or instant gratification) will offer us greater rewards in the long run.

Larger goals can be achieved through the incremental steps of achieving smaller goals. Stay diligent, persevere, and take consistent steps to stay on track to achieving your greater goals in life.

Cultivating Good Habits for Sustainable Progress

Good habits are integral to sustainable progress because they help us to form foundations that are consistent and reliable. They provide a platform from which we can reliably reach our goals and make steady progress over time.

These habits could be establishing a proper sleep schedule, eating nutritious food, exercising regularly, and maintaining positive relationships with others – all essential components of leading a healthy life. Without good habits, it becomes difficult to sustain meaningful progress over any length of time.

One of the best ways to cultivate good habits is to start small and focus on one or two at a time, rather than trying to adopt many new habits at once. For example, if you want to start eating healthier, focus on adding more fruits and vegetables into your diet rather than completely overhauling your meal plan overnight. Additionally, it helps to set specific goals with achievable deadlines so that you stay motivated and make measurable progress toward achieving them.

For our efforts in cultivating good habits to bear fruit, we need discipline and commitment. As Aristotle famously said, *"We are what we repeatedly do. Excellence then is not an act, but a habit."* To ensure that we remain consistent in our efforts and stay focused on our goals, even when things don't go according to plan, inspiration and motivation from role models who have achieved great things through their hard work and dedication can be invaluable sources of strength and guidance for others striving for excellence in their own lives.

In addition to establishing good habits, it is also important to manage bad habits and practice restraint when necessary. Initially, it may seem that some bad habits are harmless, but they can quickly become addictions if ignored. A smoking or drinking habit, for example, can cause health problems in the long run. Discipline and self-control are key in this regard and require conscious effort.

Cultivating good habits can help individuals to realise their full potential and sustainably progress toward their desired goals without damaging their health or affecting others negatively. It takes discipline and commitment to stick to good practices every day, but such habits ultimately lead to greater contentment in life.

New Opportunities

"Life is too short to settle for mediocrity. The world waits for those courageous enough to take risks, create new opportunities and grow themselves and those around them. If one does not build bridges of improvement, then life quickly passes us by without very much progress." – Seneca, On The Shortness of Life, 49AD.

How often in life do we find ourselves settling, either out of fear or comfort? We may think that we have found a place where we feel secure and content, only to realise later that there is still so much more to be gained from our time on Earth. Instead of staying complacent in the same spot, we must strive for growth and improvement every day by creating new opportunities for ourselves. Ajeet risked complacency in his comfortable life but managed to find a new opportunity through his reflections. The takeaway message here is clear: don't just settle when there is so much opportunity all around you. Choose to use each moment as an opportunity for growth and improvement; choose to continuously create new opportunities for yourself without hesitation or fear;

choose to keep discovering what you can achieve, just as Seneca himself did throughout his lifetime.

Wise words from Marie Curie remind us that, *"Nothing in life is to be feared, it is only to be understood. Now is the time to understand more so that we may fear less."* It can be daunting to take risks and venture out into unknown territory, but with knowledge comes power. If we take enough time to properly research our options before taking a leap of faith, then the chances are high that we will be successful.

This thought was shared by Seneca thousands of years ago, and still holds true today. We must be proactive about creating the conditions we need for growth and embracing the changes we need to make to improve our lives. Whether it's personal development, career advancement, or just general wellbeing, if we are not continuously striving to better ourselves and our situation, then we will find ourselves standing still as life moves on.

Thomas Edison once famously said, *"Opportunity is missed by most people because it is dressed in overalls and looks like work."* Even when faced with hard work, it is important to remember that through hard work comes reward, both in terms of tangible rewards such as monetary gain, and also intangible rewards such as feeling satisfied that you have taken positive steps toward achieving your life's goals.

The writer Anais Nin noted that, *"Life shrinks or expands in proportion to one's courage."* When we take a risk and push forward with something new against all odds, we are often rewarded with exciting opportunities that would otherwise never have presented themselves. It takes courage to break away from the status quo, but doing so can bring about far greater rewards than expected, making any hardships seem worthwhile in hindsight.

Don't settle for mediocrity. Instead, go out there, create new opportunities, seize them, and make each moment count!

Lessons from Seizing Opportunities

Reflection provides clarity to understand yourself better, enabling you to uncover fresh perspectives on familiar problems or challenges that otherwise may have stagnated.

Courage can be seen as a prerequisite for success. Without a willingness to take risks or make changes, there can be no hope of moving forward.

Change allows you to act upon fresh perspectives and seize new opportunities. It can be seen as a catalyst for personal development. By being open to new possibilities, you can emerge stronger than ever before.

By understanding your own desires and values, and staying true to them even when faced with adversity or temptation, you can make meaningful progress toward achieving authentic success.

By completing smaller tasks now that contribute to your overall larger, future goal, you will create your path toward long-term success. Find ways to play the long game while embracing each moment life brings you.

Adversities may not always be negative, or if they are, others have overcome them and will be able to guide you through. Uncertainty and adversity are a part of life out with your control, but how you respond to them is within your control, so channel your energies wisely.

Don't be afraid of failure because it is the lessons learned that help propel you forward in life. Embrace failure as an opportunity to grow stronger and smarter. Be brave at taking risks and trying new things, fail well, and learn from your mistakes.

Larger goals can be achieved through the incremental steps of achieving smaller goals. Stay diligent, persevere, and take consistent steps to stay on track to achieving your greater goals in life.

Cultivating good habits can help you realise your full potential and sustainably progress toward your desired goals. It takes discipline and commitment to stick to good practices every day, but such habits ultimately lead to greater contentment in life.

Don't settle for mediocrity. Instead, go out there, create new opportunities, seize them, and make each moment count!

Chapter 5

Never Too Late for Happiness

Leo had been living a mundane life for far too long. For years, his days were filled with the same routine; going to work, coming home, watching some television, and sleeping. It was a cycle that left him feeling unfulfilled and drained of energy. He had grown lethargic and overweight, and he had little joy in life.

One day while walking through the city, Leo noticed an old man, walking slowly with his stick. Everyone around the old man was busy and rushed, frowning or dazed. Something about this man struck Leo as different from all the other people who were going about their lives in a robotic way. He stopped to take a closer look and noticed the old man wore an air of contentment about him that seemed out of place amidst all the chaos around him. He was smiling and calm; he was content. Intrigued, Leo approached him, and asked why he was so content.

The old man smiled at him and replied, "It's never too late to change your life." Leo was sure there must be more to whatever secret the old man had discovered, but he thanked him and walked on.

Reflecting on the old man's words, Leo, although in his fifties, contemplated how he could change his life to find contentment without sacrificing what security he had. Should he change his career? Should he move home, or break off his relationship with his partner?

He couldn't see how changing these things would improve his life. And then one day, something clicked: perhaps he could start with something small and make incremental changes in his life. Perhaps small changes would become meaningful over time, and improve his life more significantly with time.

So, Leo chose two new habits to focus on. These were reading books and walking once a week to help him stay healthy and active. He soon found himself chatting to people about what he was reading and decided to join a local book reading club. He made new friends, connecting with them over their shared love of reading. He also wondered about joining a walking club, but after discovering there wasn't one in his area, he made the decision to start one. He took leaflets around to his neighbours telling them about what he planned to do and inviting them to join him. He soon heard from a few who were interested and keen to go walking, feeling they would be more likely to do so in a group. Again, Leo made new friends, improving his physical health in the process. Others heard about his walking group and joined too. They told him how their own health had improved since they started walking with him, meaning Leo felt a certain satisfaction from supporting the activity not only for himself, but also for others. This gave his life meaning and brought him happiness.

Over time, these changes brought feelings of joy and purpose that had been missing from his life – not because they were necessarily life-changing choices but because they were meaningful to Leo. They showed him that nothing is set in stone, and he had the power to create his own destiny through his own decisions and actions.

Inspired by this newfound empowerment, Leo realised that it was never too late to change his life. The old man had been right. He just needed to make up his mind to do so, and he could choose to do so at any age.

Control Your Happiness

Happiness is an elusive concept, and we often wonder why it eludes us. Seneca believed, *"It is not the man who has too little, but the man who craves more, that is poor."* It is never too late to take control of your happiness. But, to do so, you need to assess your desires and needs in life, make decisions, and act on them.

It takes work and effort to bring about lasting change and true joy in life. At any age, you can look for ways to engage with the world that bring you contentment. Identify and invest in hobbies or activities that you enjoy. These will serve you better than pursuits like watching television for entertainment; such activities lead to short-term gratification and may have a negative impact on your health.

Taking control of your own happiness is one of the most important lessons you can learn. Seneca said, *"If you want to be happy, no one can stop you."* The responsibility for your own joy lies within you, and it is up to you to take charge and live life with intention.

Leo took charge of his life and changed it. He did this by starting two new hobbies, and he succeeded in becoming healthier *and* finding happiness through his new interests and the connections he made with others. By setting goals in line with your personal values and striving toward creating an authentic life filled with meaning, you will take control of your own happiness.

For centuries, people have echoed the same advice: find a way to make yourself content and at peace with who you are and what you have. Take time out from searching for external sources of fulfilment and you will find that happiness often comes from inside. Leo found his interests from within himself; nobody else could find them for him.

American psychotherapist Dr Carl Rogers advocated for self-actualisation. He described this as "becoming fully aware of what you want out of life – understanding yourself and allowing your fullest potentials to be expressed through creative activities or personal relationships." This can be liberating because instead of seeking approval from outside sources such as family or peers, focus shifts toward finding internal satisfaction that comes from being true to yourself while connecting with others authentically.

Only you know what would make you content, and only you can make the decisions and take the actions to find that contentment. So, if you are not content at any age, consider what would make you happy, and what decisions or actions you need to take to realise that happiness. Take control of your happiness.

Don't be Held Back

Every one of us has experienced moments in life when something (or someone) has held us back from achieving our goals. We might be held back by fear, insecurity, or a lack of confidence – all highly debilitating emotions. But it may also be an outside force such as a difficult person in your life who undermines you and dislikes you for no good reason. In either case, understanding what is holding you back and then having the courage to just let go can often release a floodgate of new potential and opportunities that may have previously seemed out of reach. In other words, understand what is holding you back and then learn to let go if you want to get ahead and make the most of life. American author Toni Morrison addressed this concept with the words, *"You wanna fly, you gotta give up the stuff that holds you down."* And it's never too late to let go of whatever is holding you back.

Nelson Mandela once said, *"It always seems impossible until it is done."* His words inspired countless listeners to push through their inner fears and find creative solutions to overcome obstacles in their lives. No matter how insurmountable something might seem at first, with enough passion and determination, there is always a way forward.

Life is short and there are few things more valuable than understanding what is holding you back. You need to become aware of what is standing in your way to be able to find a way through or around it. Lao Tzu said, *"When I let go of what I am, I become what I might be."* In essence, this quote conveys how letting go of the limitations (often self-imposed) that are holding you back can open up unlimited opportunities for you.

One of the most powerful tools for helping us to understand what is holding us back is the practice of mindfulness. Mindfulness helps us develop greater awareness of our thoughts and feelings, allowing us to identify the source of our anxiety or fear so we can take steps to let it go. This allows us to find peace in the present moment instead of worrying about past mistakes or future worries. As Gandhi once said, *"The moment you dispute your own mind, you enter into the peace zone."*

One way to understand and overcome what is holding you back is through reflecting on your actions and recognising patterns. Writing a journal can help you with this process by providing an opportunity to document day-to-day experiences so you can analyse them later. This reflective process allows you to identify patterns in the way you think and act that may be destructive. Identifying these habits enables you to start making conscious choices that will lead toward freedom from damaging behaviours.

Seeking advice from individuals who have already travelled down the path you wish to take can also be invaluable when trying to release whatever is holding you back. By listening attentively and truly considering the insight of experienced advisers, you can gain clarity on why you may be getting stuck, or how best to move forward with courage. As philosopher John Dewey wrote: *"The insight enabling one person's life by illuminating its difficulties is sometimes gained only through intimate contact with another's life as seen in its joys and dangers."*

In conclusion, understanding what holds you back in life offers an important opportunity for growth and transformation. You need to let go of fears before they restrict your progress. By using mindfulness practices, reflecting on past experiences, and engaging in thoughtful conversations with wise mentors, you will be able to live authentically. It's never too late to identify, bring into full view, and cast away the obstacles that are holding you back.

Don't Compare Yourself to Others

To quote Steve Jobs: "Your time is limited, so don't waste it living someone else's life." Comparing yourself to others is a foolish act. It denies your own reality to strive toward an idealised version of yourself. As someone wise once said, *"Another's activity makes no man more active; another's danger does not make you braver."* Recognise that other people's successes are theirs and understand that measuring your own progress against theirs is counterproductive.

We are commonly taught to compare our achievements and milestones against those of peers and acquaintances. We are always pushing for more, and measuring success by how quickly we reach those goals, making it easy to forget the value of taking time to appreciate your personal growth and development. Taking longer to accomplish something compared to someone else isn't important, all that's important is that you've accomplished it – one step at a time. Seneca wrote extensively on his belief that people should strive for individual growth instead of focusing on what everyone else is doing. He believed that we should not let ourselves be limited by those around us, and should instead focus on achieving personal excellence.

"Although life is short, it offers us plenty of opportunity for greatness, if we make the right use of it." – Seneca, On the Shortness of Life, 49AD. In this statement, Seneca is suggesting that the amount of time we have should not stop us from achieving great things, implying that it is up to each individual person to make the most of their unique situation. We must understand that life moves at its own pace and will only offer what is needed when it is needed.

Theodore Roosevelt said, *"Comparison is the thief of joy,"* and Eleanor Roosevelt added weight to this when she said, *"No one can make you feel inferior without your consent."* These wise words serve to demonstrate how vital it is that you don't rely on external factors or comparisons to maintain your sense of worth, or allow other people's opinions to shape your destiny. Comparing yourself to others and their achievements may seem like an effective way to motivate yourself and spur growth, but all too often it only serves as a debilitating force. Taking stock of your progress in comparison to others can be emotionally damaging and lead you away from a meaningful and rewarding life.

Life's journey involves failures as well as successes, and while others may appear to be progressing faster than you, they too have experienced difficulties along their paths to reach where they are today. For this reason, the goal should not be to race toward an end goal, but to commit to self-improvement and personal achievement at any stage, any age, and in any way possible. By adopting a mindset of appreciation rather than comparison, we can embrace our unique journey with faith and understanding.

The concept of delayed gratification is key here. While it may be tempting to compare yourself to those who achieved success quicker than you, it's important to keep in mind that real success takes time. Impulsive short-term decisions will often take you down paths that may lead to momentary joys, but ultimately yield inferior results. Your accomplishments are only truly worthwhile if they come from effort over an extended period of time. As Warren Buffet said, *"Successful investing takes time, discipline and patience."* Success is not age dependent, it's possible at any age. Your journey must be your own. You must accept your current possibilities and develop patience for what will come in the future. This isn't easy, but it's of far greater benefit than letting yourself become overly competitive with others.

Comparing yourself with others can make you feel inadequate or discouraged, and it's likely to keep you blinkered to your own worth. Today is a new day full of possibility. Your experiences have shaped who you are today and provided insight into where you want your life to go. Both can inform how you measure yourself relative only to your past events, rather than others' accomplishments. Don't compare yourself with peers as this will limit your progress toward true fulfilment, and don't consider your age to be a barrier to achievement compared to others. Instead, understand and appreciate your own pace of growth so that you can live authentically.

Age is Not a Barrier

We often believe that age limits us, but the truth is that our potential knows no bounds. It was Abraham Lincoln who once said, *"It's not the years in your life that count. It's the life in your years,"* and the meaning in this is that it doesn't matter if you are old or young, what matters is how you live your life and how you use your time and energy.

As we age, our bodies may naturally become less capable, but this does not mean we must become complacent or set lower expectations for ourselves. Even if we face physical limitations due to age or health conditions, with creativity and grit, we can still rise to the challenge of achieving our goals.

This idea has been echoed by many distinguished thinkers throughout history. Confucius said, *"The man who says he can and the man who says he cannot are both usually right."* This is an important reminder that we should never let our perceived limitations determine our future success. Instead, we need to open ourselves up to possibility and work toward what excites us without limiting ourselves based on age.

Age may bring aches and pains, but it also opens up incredible opportunities for growth and progress as long as you remain passionate about pursuing something bigger than yourself. Remembering this will help you stay motivated despite any physical ailments or mental barriers related to aging that may appear before you on your journey.

Age should not be an excuse for not reaching your potential. You will find ways to push yourself further, explore new opportunities, and discover hidden talents. As Mark Twain voiced, *"Age is an issue of mind over matter. If you don't mind, it doesn't matter."* There are many successful people who achieve remarkable things despite their age. You need to set your expectations appropriately so that whatever your age, you never give up on reaching your goals.

Focus on your intentions and personal motivations when striving for success, regardless of your age or physical capabilities. Always look beyond what seems achievable now and aim higher by constantly challenging yourself with incremental next steps. With hard work, drive, and ambition, no one should ever let their age define them or limit their potential.

Invest in Personal Growth

Investing in your own personal growth is crucial at all ages. It isn't just essential for making the most of a finite life, it's also a rewarding process both mentally and emotionally, bringing many long-term benefits.

A great way to invest in your personal growth is through reading. Reading not only helps you learn about different subjects and potentially gain skills, it can also provide an escape from everyday life and open your mind to new ideas and perspectives. In Leo's case, he took the opportunity to share those ideas by discussing them with other members of a book club.

Another way to further your development is to keep a journal or diary. Writing down your thoughts, worries, and successes is a great way to gain clarity on what you are feeling, and to reflect upon the events in life that occur around you. Mark Twain said, *"The difference between the right word and almost the right word is like the difference between lightning and a lightning bug."* Writing can help clarify exactly how you feel about something, rather than just having an inkling about it.

Investing in yourself may involve finding mentors or coaches who can provide guidance during times when you are feeling stuck or repeatedly facing roadblocks to achieving your goals. Remember that "you are the average of the five people you spend the most time with," so having a friend with experience in a certain area may provide invaluable advice and insight that would be difficult to find elsewhere.

A key aspect of personal growth is identifying and reflecting on your strengths and weaknesses. Author Elle Luna suggests, *"We can only take responsibility for our lives when we recognise where we stand right now and accept ourselves just as we are."* Making an honest inventory of who you are and how you can improve allows you to focus your energy and resources on creating meaningful change. Leo's reflections on the possibility of changing his career, home, or relationship led him to realise changing those things would not bring happiness. Reflections on feeling unfulfilled in life did however lead him to change his habits and behaviour, and those changes introduced new hobbies that brought new meaning and purpose.

Deliberate practice and hard work are also necessary ingredients for investing in your personal growth. The key here is to make small strides toward achieving your goals. Practicing an instrument regularly, for example, will eventually result in major improvement in your musical skills. Leo first started reading, and then joined a club. He started walking, and then decided to start a walking club. A first step to starting a walking club was to design a leaflet to distribute locally to people who might be interested in joining him. The leaflet didn't accomplish his goal of setting up a walking club, but it was the first step toward that goal.

Investing in your personal growth is an undertaking that requires dedication and perseverance. This must be ongoing, and can therefore be practiced at any age, bringing immense rewards that help you to achieve great potential. Consider reading, diary writing, reflecting on your experiences, and finding mentors to help your personal growth. Personal development will require deliberate practice and hard work, but tackling small steps and taking them one at a time will result in long-term gains. It may take years for the fruits of this labour to ripen, but when they do, it will be worth all the effort you put into changing yourself.

Start Something New

The value of starting something new has been appreciated throughout history by many thought leaders, and it's something that is possible at any age. Leo took up the hobbies of reading and walking in his fifties and these small changes in his life reaped great rewards. His life became fulfilled through the happiness his new interests brought him, and the new connections he made with others.

The idea of starting something new carries with it a certain power that can be harnessed for great reward. As Albert Einstein once said, *"In the middle of difficulty lies opportunity."* When you embark on a journey into uncharted territory, you are presented with challenges and obstacles that offer unique opportunities for growth and learning if taken advantage of in the right way. Leo wanted to join a walking group but was faced with the challenge of no group existing in his local area. He saw this challenge as an opportunity to start his own group.

Starting something new also brings its own set of benefits, such as having control over your life and being able to shape your own future. Through hard work and determination, anything we set our minds to can be achieved – no matter what it may be.

Age is no barrier. You can start something new at any stage in life, and the challenges you meet on the journey may turn into opportunities. Starting something new brings new powers that will help you to shape your future.

Opportunities in Every Situation

Life is short, and time passes quickly. Before you know it, another opportunity presents itself that you can take advantage of. This realisation was at the heart of Seneca's words when he said, *"Look for opportunity in every situation."*

Seizing opportunities requires an attitude of bravery and curiosity. You should strive for new perspectives and gutsy ideas instead of giving in to fear or uncertainty. Every moment contains a unique possibility. Recognising this takes courage, but its rewards can be immense. This has been impressively demonstrated by those who have achieved great things despite hardship or injustice throughout history. Individuals such as Rosa Parks, Nelson Mandela, and Malala Yousafzai are true examples of leaders whose courage changed their lives – and the world around them – forever.

Seneca reminds us that even seemingly tragic circumstances hold opportunities just waiting to be unlocked, if only we open ourselves up to possibility rather than clinging on too tightly to preconceived notions about how life should unfold according to plans. Life's most meaningful moments come from learning how to look below the surface for fresh perspectives on familiar situations and immersing yourself fully in those new discoveries.

Australian psychologist Matt Church echoes this sentiment in saying, *"Sometimes life will present you with difficult challenges that can feel too hard or overwhelming... [But] they also provide opportunities for growth and learning if you let them."* Good opportunities can present themselves unexpectedly, even during times when we least expect it, so it pays to remain open-minded and proactive when facing any challenge or difficulty.

No matter how dire things may seem, there are always possibilities hidden within difficulty; we just need the right perspective and courage to explore them. When faced with struggle, instead of focusing on failures or drawbacks in your current circumstances, look around for possible sources of success, even in places where none may seem visible at first glance. Difficulties give birth to extraordinary achievements.

By embracing this outlook on life, you can start uncovering unexpected possibilities even from what initially appeared to be an impossibility, thereby living up to Seneca's famous dictum: *"Luck is what happens when preparation meets opportunity."*

Small Steps

Life is long if you know how to use it. In his book, On the Shortness of Life, published in 49AD, Seneca uses his own experiences and reflections on life to illustrate how having a purposeful yet balanced approach to living can make all the difference in achieving your goals.

This concept continues to echo through the words of modern-day thought leaders and entrepreneurs, including Tim Ferriss. In his book, The 4-Hour Workweek, published in 2007, he says, *"Focus on being productive instead of busy. Constrain your time but expand your output... Start with essentials first, then add optional tasks if you have more time."* Setting achievable yet challenging goals and ensuring productivity from them allows optimum results to be achieved regardless of limitations in time.

Setting aside just a few minutes each day for self-improvement activities is essential to lead a successful and rewarding life. As Marcus Aurelius said, *"If thou workest at what is before thee... What nature requireth of thee will be fulfilled, spending no thought upon future things."* Not everything you need to accomplish to reach your goals will be possible today, but by focusing your efforts on what is right in front of you – almost like pieces of a puzzle slowly coming together – you can eventually form something far greater than you anticipated when you began your journey.

Tony Robbins puts it this way: *"The path to success is to take massive, determined action."* However, this doesn't mean taking huge leaps every single day, it means taking small steps every day – consistently and determinedly – so that achievable action is a daily habit, *every* day. Each tiny step may seem insignificant in the moment, but over time these small steps can make all the difference in terms of achieving your goals.

Making progress on any task starts with breaking it down into smaller chunks. Having a clear plan of what needs to be done each day allows you to really focus on making steady progress. In his book, Getting Things Done, published in 2001, Dave Allen wrote, *"You can do anything, but not everything."* Even minor improvements and tweaks each day add up quickly, leading you ever closer to the finish line.

Swami Vivekananda gives similar advice: *"Take up one idea. Make that one idea your life – think of it, dream of it, live on that idea."* Taking action on your goals can give you the motivation to move forward, knowing that even small steps are progress toward your larger goals. The truth is that success rarely happens overnight but rather occurs after taking many small steps over time. This highlights the importance of starting somewhere, no matter how small or insignificant the step may seem, because it is the first step towards achieving your goal. There can be no progress if you don't start.

A journey of a thousand miles begins with a single step. This old proverb can be applied to journeying through life and achieving goals. Taking small steps each day can help develop essential habits needed for success, such as discipline, resilience, and determination, while also helping you move closer to your end goal.

Little things make big things happen. So, remember, it doesn't matter how big or small your daily actions are, every action counts and brings you closer to achieving your goals.

Believing in Yourself

Believe in yourself and all that you can achieve. This age-old saying is a great reminder that to really understand who you are, and to reach your full potential, you need to have faith in yourself and what you can achieve. Maya Angelou pointed out how crucial this self-belief is when she said, *"You can't expect someone else to believe in you, if you don't believe in yourself."*

Belief gives you the inner strength to get back up when you fall, but it's more than bounce-back-ability, it's recognising your strengths even when faced with adversity or uncertainty. *"Our greatest glory lies not in never falling but in rising every time we fall."*

Believing in yourself and all that you can achieve is a fundamental part of living the fullest life. Every one of us has an impressive power to create our own destiny by staying true to ourselves and believing in what we can do. We should recognise our strengths and use them courageously to set our goals, take risks, think positively, and above all else, never give up hope. It's only through believing in ourselves that we unlock the power to solve our current obstacles and transform our lives for the better.

If you don't believe something is possible then it won't be possible. Belief in yourself is something that can be developed over time through practice and dedication, but it must begin with your thoughts about yourself. Albert Einstein believed every person was capable of greatness. He said, *"Everyone is a genius, but if you judge a fish by its ability to climb a tree, it will live its whole life thinking it's stupid."* His words demonstrate how valuable self-belief is, but also how society can often stifle natural potential by placing expectations on people that may not fit their skillsets or future desires.

Ultimately, believing in yourself means being brave enough to confront fears, to be honest about who you are, to appreciate what you already have, and to persevere with your dreams, no matter how big or small those dreams may be. Don't be afraid! Have faith in yourself and trust that you will succeed no matter what obstacles stand before you.

Let Go of Perfectionism

The concept of striving for perfection can be detrimental and cause unnecessary stress in your life. We are all imperfect beings and should embrace our weaknesses, using them as opportunities to learn and grow. Constantly seeking an idealistic version of yourself can be emotionally exhausting and lead you down the road of self-sabotage. Letting go of perfectionism is an essential part of living a life full of meaning and purpose. It takes practice, but once achieved offers immense rewards both mentally and physically.

Perfectionists tend to focus too much on minor details. This not only delays their progress, it also means they tend to become overwhelmed with feelings of disappointment and failure when they don't meet their self-imposed impossibly high standards. Taking action rather than becoming stuck in endless self-doubt or worrying about imperfections – real or perceived – is crucial to self-improvement and striving for excellence. Aviation pioneer Amelia Earhart once said, *"The most difficult thing is the decision to act; the rest is merely tenacity."* As soon as you take action, everything else will start falling into place. Of course, mistakes will happen along the way, but these should be seen as an opportunity for growth instead of an indication of failure or inferiority.

Focusing on progress, rather than perfection, allows you to accept yourself as you are without putting extra pressure on yourself to be perfect. Being released from the need for perfection allows you to explore new ideas, take risks, create meaningful relationships with other people, enjoy life experiences, and learn from past mistakes. By letting perfectionism go, you will happily accept your own personal version of excellence! Excellence can be achieved instead by focusing on developing skills, growing as an individual, and making a positive impact by taking bold action. Mark Twain put this into words by saying, *"When we strive to become better than we are, everything around us becomes better too."* Striving for excellence brings both short-term rewards, such as feeling proud at the end of a challenging project, and long-term rewards, such as a career achievement or the knowledge gained from learning something new.

To truly maximise your potential, you must accept your flaws and work toward being the best version of yourself. Letting go of perfectionism allows you to move forward with confidence, take bold actions, and find success through hard work and determination

Lessons from Never Too Late for Happiness

Take control of your happiness! Consider what would make you happy, and what decisions and actions would help you to realise that happiness.

Identify and cast away the obstacles that are holding you back by practicing mindfulness, reflecting on past experiences, and engaging in thoughtful conversations with wise mentors. You will then be able to live authentically.

Your goals, progress, pace, and accomplishments are unique to you and your life, so don't compare yourself with others. Measure yourself only relative to your own past.

Don't let your age define you or limit your potential. Focus on your intentions and personal motivations when striving for success, regardless of your age or physical capabilities.

Investing in your personal growth is valuable at any age; the rewards are immense and will help you achieve great potential. Consider reading, diary writing, reflecting on your experiences, and finding mentors to help your personal growth.

You can start something new at any age, and the challenges you meet on the journey may turn into opportunities. Starting something new brings new powers that will help you to shape your future.

Look for new opportunities everywhere, even in misfortune.

Take regular small steps toward your goals. Every action toward a goal, however small, brings you closer to achieving it.

Believe in yourself and trust that you will succeed, no matter what obstacles stand before you.

Let go of perfectionism, accept your flaws, take bold actions, and work toward being the best version of yourself!

Chapter 6

Death Comes Quickly

Robert had been looking forward to his wedding day since the moment he popped the question. Little did he know that his special day was about to take a drastic turn.

Just two hours after saying 'I do,' he was in hospital with four drips in his arms being told he had type 1 diabetes, something very uncommon for someone his age (40). For Robert, this felt like a cruel twist of fate, but he refused to give up hope.

The circumstances surrounding his diagnosis served as an important reminder of just how precious life is and how quickly death can come. The doctor confided that if Robert's wife – of a couple of hours – hadn't phoned 999 when she did, there was a strong chance he could have gone into a diabetic coma. It made him realise just how much time he'd wasted taking life for granted. Now he wanted to make the most of every single day.

Robert's new philosophy on life is that diabetes saved his life. Before his diagnosis, he took life for granted, but now he seizes every day to live a fuller life. His health scare taught him to appreciate each moment, and this is something that inspires those around him too, always reminding his family and friends not to take life for granted. Because death comes quicker than we realise, it's important that we seize the day: *carpe diem.*

Live Well Before Death Finds You

This might sound morbid, but every day we are running toward death, whether we like it or not. No man can avoid its inescapable presence in this system of things. To ensure that the time we have remaining is worthwhile, fleeing from death's grasp should be a priority for us all. Though it may seem daunting to escape such a powerful force, Seneca reminds us that if we recognise our mortality and act accordingly, although we can't avoid death, we can use the knowledge of our mortality to our advantage.

Happiness and contentment are all within reach so long as we learn how to prioritise the life that has been gifted to us by improving our perspective and mindset on life itself. As former President Barack Obama once said, *"We may not be able to control the length of our lives, but we can always control its width, its breadth, and its depth."* The key to living a fulfilling life is therefore to find ways to maximise the width, breadth and depth of our lives – its richness – and to avoid wasting it on trivial pursuits or pessimism.

One way to recognise life's richness is through understanding that all moments count in life – even the mundane ones – and genuinely enjoying them while they last. As Mark Twain noted, *"Life doesn't need any improvement; every day as it comes adds something fresh and new. You should never wish away any day until after it has gone…That would deprive you of much pleasure and miss many surprises which might have been in store for you."* Our minds provide us with an array of opportunities for making these special moments part of our everyday existence. For example, you can read books from different perspectives, learn a new language, spend quality time with loved ones, or take a leisurely walk outside to enjoy nature's beauty. These are all activities that provide unique experiences and add character and colour to your life story.

Living intentionally will also help you to flee from death before it finds you. Being mindful helps you to identify what matters most in your life and to avoid wasting time on things that won't bring lasting satisfaction or meaningful memories. Meaningful memories can be built over time by building relationships or by nourishing your inner spirit with activities such as writing, gardening, or anything else that you love doing. And, it doesn't matter if others don't approve of your choice of activities. Steve Jobs captured this succinctly when he pointed out that life is short and that you need to ensure you don't waste it trying to live someone else's version of what life should be like for you. The Dalai Lama added to this when he said, *"Do not let the behaviour of others destroy your inner peace."* Life is too precious for this kind of negativity; instead, embrace life now while you still can. Ultimately, your choice of activities and personal self-improvement will allow you greater freedom in terms of your fate. Death will only find you after you have found a purposeful and meaningful existence. Make sure that your time on Earth is well spent, and that you are truly living with purpose. As Eleanor Roosevelt once said, *"The purpose of life is to live it, to taste experience to the utmost, to reach out eagerly and without fear for newer and richer experiences."* Don't allow yourself to drift through life. Choose to use your short time here purposefully.

Seneca also argued that while death can catch up with any of us at any age or stage in life, life can also surprise us by going beyond its normal course. It sometimes happens that life may be prolonged, even against nature's law. This means that even when confronted with the inevitability of death, we should take full advantage of every moment given to us. There may be more time than you think!

This way of looking at life can also help people stay present and in touch with their surroundings, never taking anything for granted or wasting an opportunity. In essence, Seneca believed that fleeing from death before it finds you falls within everyone's power. The key is to remain mindful of your mortality and imbue meaning and joy into every moment rather than meaningless drudgery or despair.

"When you arise in the morning, think of what a privilege it is to be alive... to breathe, to think, to enjoy, to love." Spoken by Marcus Aurelius in 180AD, these words serve as a reminder that fleeing from death before it finds you means learning how best to make use of precious moments now, rather than letting such moments pass by unnoticed or on poorly chosen activities. It means appreciating every experience, however small. Recognise mortality and work intentionally toward attaining happiness in whatever shape or form it takes *now* – not at some point down the road when your days may already be numbered.

Futility of Worry

What good does fretting about the future do? If your days are limited anyway, why not focus on living them to their fullest potential instead? Seneca believed that worrying was futile since all worries came with an expiration date. At one point or another all those worries will become meaningless as soon as their cause passes away with time.

Life is brief, and it passes quickly. Worry and fear are futile emotions; they only lead to distress, sadness, and despair. As Seneca wrote, *"We suffer more in imagination than in reality."* To truly appreciate life's brevity, you need to accept what you can't control and focus your energy on what can be changed for the better.

French philosopher Montaigne echoed this sentiment when he wrote: *"Our life is composed greatly from dreams, from the future, and expectations."* This reminds us to live in the present moment and to remain conscious of how quickly days pass us by. Henry David Thoreau added to this when he said, *"Time is but the stream I go a-fishing in."* The river of life runs quickly and carries us along with its current. As we drift downstream toward death, our time spent worrying about inconsequential matters means nothing at all.

Being mindful of life's brevity enables us to make every moment meaningful. As Marcus Aurelius so eloquently voiced, *"It always remains a simple summary – remember how swiftly things pass away!" Let us treasure each second as if it were our last, because one day soon enough it will be just that."*

William Shakespeare shared this sentiment when he wrote: *"Our revels now are ended. These our actors, as I foretold you, were all spirits and are melted into air, into thin air. And like the baseless fabric of this vision, the cloud-capp'd towers, the gorgeous palaces, the solemn temples, the great globe itself... all which it inherits shall dissolve."*

The brevity of life resonates with all of us on some level, even if many of us do not fully appreciate it until later in life, or until death has taken its toll on someone close to us. But worry can also rob us of valuable time that could have been better spent savouring and enjoying the moments we have here with those we love, or pursuing meaningful goals or ambitions.

Seneca wrote about worry extensively in his letters and believed that worry could not be outrun because it lies within and can consume your thoughts regardless of where you find yourself in life. He asserted that worrying was useless because it doesn't change what will happen or help you control your fate. However, it does rob you of a certain amount of peace, day by day. Seneca implored individuals to focus more on changing their state of mind rather than external circumstances as a method for managing anxiety. In Letters From A Stoic, published in 69AD, he wrote, *"Take heart then; rise superior to this tempestuous sea; an armed man can meet such things – no weapon more useful – arm yourself with strength! To fight against fortune is folly but to govern your spirit is wisdom!"*

Helen Keller described worry as a "small trickle of fear that meanders through the mind until it cuts a channel

so wide that all other thoughts are drained away."
Further, she explained that worrying does nothing but
erode our mental energy, leaving little else for productive
or creative activities.

John Muir wrote about worry in reference to nature. He
said, *"Climb the mountains and get their good tidings –
nature's peace will flow into you as sunshine flows into
trees... In every walk in nature, one receives far more than
[s]he seeks."* He saw nature not only as a refuge from fear
and worry but also as a means of promoting growth and
self-discovery, providing solace when most needed.

Modern-day philosopher Alan Watts has added, *"Rather
than being your thoughts and emotions, be the awareness
behind them."* By remaining aware throughout your day-
to-day existence, possibilities in every moment will
emerge. By embracing what life has to offer right now
instead of delaying over fears or anxieties about an
uncertain future, you will be choosing joy rather than
suffering or sadness.

These wise minds have all recognised how debilitating
worry can be, draining away time, mental energy, joy,
and potential, while reducing capacity for meaningful
actions and interactions with others. Life is indeed
short, yet infinitely precious. Have courage and let go of
needless worries. Instead, make conscious choices to
spend each fleeting moment on Earth wisely.

Embrace Life Now

Seizing the present and making use of it efficiently is
essential if you want stability in life over the course of

its limited duration. If you live in the past or look too far ahead into an unpredictable future, you will lose sight of what's most important: the present moment! Seneca, through his wise words, implores us to take pleasure in living presently without fearing death. If you live in this way, you have already achieved abundance before your physical demise.

Walt Disney once said, *"The way to get started is to quit talking and begin doing."* You need to take action now! Don't wait for something great to come along; make things happen yourself. Life is short, so don't waste any time stressing about potential outcomes or obsessing over details beyond your control, just enjoy each moment and make the best out of each situation that comes your way.

We are all part of a vast expanse of energy that ebbs and flows with time. The days pass quickly and before we know it, life is almost gone. This reality can be disconcerting, so the best thing we can do is embrace life while it's still here. Don't wait until you are diagnosed with diabetes like Robert, or with some other life-changing illness, change your life for the better *now.*

In the midst of chaos or sorrow there will always be something to hold onto if you remain open enough to find it. A smile from someone on the street; a song you used to love playing as background music; a simple sunset viewed through an old windowpane… All these moments become extraordinarily special if appreciated from within each present second. When you learn to accept joy even amidst sadness, then more beautiful moments magically appear out of nowhere. You will realise what is truly valuable in your life here on Earth. So, live in the present, take action now, and learn to appreciate all that life offers you.

Take Control of Your Destiny

Each day brings new opportunities but its own set of limits that cannot be circumvented, even with ambition or hard work. You therefore need to use this knowledge to plan out your life strategically. According to Seneca, taking control over your destiny starts by understanding how fleeting life is and leveraging this wisdom when making decisions to help achieve your goals in the time you have.

Make decisions about how you want to use your time by considering what would bring meaning and fulfilment into your life. Do work you are passionate about, learn something new, or pursue creative outlets. These can all be part of intentionally exploring what brings you joy. By committing yourself to daily acts of kindness or service toward others, you can also add immeasurable value to both your own life and the lives of those around you.

Aristotle argued, *"The energy of the mind is the essence of life."* Meaningful accomplishments begin with having the drive and determination to make something happen. Self-discipline plays an important role in managing your time appropriately and productively. Learn how to focus on your primary goals while avoiding distractions that can take you away from working toward your objectives.

Charles Schwab has suggested three steps to overcome procrastination. One: set specific goals that you want to achieve. Two: break them down into smaller tasks. And three: assign these tasks over different days so that you don't become overwhelmed by their size or importance. Doing this will help you stay organised and motivated as you work through your goals, and avoid potentially pushing them aside because they seem too daunting.

Warren Buffet said, *"If you don't find time for what's most important, then you won't be able to accomplish anything meaningful."* To truly take control of your destiny, you must learn how to prioritise projects that help you achieve your aspirations over those that merely consume your valuable resources.

Taking control of your destiny involves utilising your time wisely to make progress toward meaningful accomplishments. Remember, life may seem short, but it contains plenty of opportunities for success if managed properly. Taking control of your destiny begins by understanding the importance and true value of time. Each day that passes by is an opportunity to create new memories, experiences, or progress in some way. All too often, people's lives are filled with distractions and obligations that prevent them from focusing on their long-term goals or ambitions. The key to unlocking the beauty of life is to create balance between what you must do and what you want to do.

Richard Branson shared this insight when he said, *"Time is your most precious commodity; guard it as if your life depends on it, because it almost certainly does."* To be successful in any endeavour – personal or professional – you must learn how to prioritise your time effectively to accomplish your goals and maximise efficiency.

Making the most of your time requires discipline in allocating available hours for activities that have both short-term and long-term benefits. This means having a plan for each day and whenever possible, staying committed to pursuing projects that bring meaningful results. If you have been trying endlessly for months with no significant progress, then it might be beneficial to step away from the task temporarily until you can reassess your approach from a fresh perspective.

To summarise, taking control of your destiny requires recognising how fleeting life is, managing your time with self-discipline, identifying and prioritising meaningful activities, breaking down tasks into manageable and achievable subtasks, and avoiding distractions. While you need to plan to achieve your goals, you may also need to step back sometimes to reassess your approach from a fresh perspective.

Improve Your Life Every Day

How you are using your time is one way to evaluate how much progress you are making in terms of making meaningful improvements – so ask yourself how you are using your time every single day! What have you done today to make yourself better? How can you use your precious moments for more meaningful activities? These reflections will help you evaluate where you stand in terms of improving yourself overall.

There are many things that can be done to improve your life every day. Cultivate positive habits and routines that serve as the building blocks for success. Set aside time for meaningful relationships, take regular breaks throughout the day, and create systems to manage tasks. All these strategies can create a major impact in the long run.

Additionally, establishing healthy practices around nutrition and exercise can lead to greater wellbeing in both mind and body. Do activities you enjoy and challenge yourself by learning something new each day. Engage in mindful activities like meditation or yoga which help boost relaxation levels and increase focus and concentration on tasks.

Rather than spending too much time on meaningless pursuits, or worrying about things outside your control, focus your energy on cultivating an attitude of gratitude for the good things already present in your life, whether that is family relationships, your job, or simply having access to basic amenities like food and shelter. Use your available resources wisely, including both money and energy, and don't take any gifts from friends or strangers for granted.

Make sure your words match your actions. Be genuine in all you say and do. Whatever improvements you seek today will contribute toward improving yourself tomorrow. Don't forget that every small action brings you one step closer to reaching your desired destination.

Looking at the work of other thought leaders can provide valuable insight into the methods they use to keep themselves on the path of improvement and success. For example, Stephen Covey once remarked, *"The key is not to prioritise what's on your schedule, but to schedule your priorities."* To improve your life, you must first determine what your priorities are and then take actionable steps toward achieving them.

Author James Allen shared this point of view when he wrote: *"You will become as small as your controlling desire, as great as your dominant ambition."* In other words, by focusing on your goals and dedicating your time and energy to things that bring you closer to your goals, you can make progress on the road to improving your life.

"Have courage for the great sorrows of life and patience for the small ones; and when you have laboriously accomplished your daily tasks, go to sleep in peace." With these words, Seneca highlighted the importance of understanding your limits when it comes to achieving self-improvement. While ambition is important and necessary to achieve success, there must also be time for rest and relaxation.

In effect, the wisdom of these thought leaders points out two important truths about improving your life: have achievable goals in mind and be consistent in pursuing them. These truths are essential components of growth and success over time. By actively practicing both, you will be well on your way toward realising a better tomorrow for yourself than was possible yesterday. Make every day count, even if you only take a small step. Be grateful for the things you already have, recognise your limits, and allow yourself rest and relaxation too.

Who Are You, and When Will You Disappear?

Developing a strong character through self-reflection and contemplating your mortality will make you impervious to death's menacing presence! Who are we and when will we disappear? This is a question that has captured the minds of thinkers for centuries, and one that continues to baffle us today. Seneca wrote: *"People look for retreats for themselves, in the country, by the coast, or in the hills… There is nowhere that a person can find a more peaceful and trouble-free retreat than in his own mind… So constantly give yourself this retreat and renew yourself."* In other words, each one of us needs to find our own refuge inside, so that no matter what life throws at us or how turbulent the times may be, we will always have a place of peace within ourselves.

Lao Tzu wrote: *"The reason why rivers and seas receive the homage of a hundred mountain streams is that they keep below them."* Similarly, if you want to live life fully and achieve success in whatever endeavour you pursue, then it is important to stay humble despite all your successes. This might sound counterintuitive, but it's essential to remember that while striving for greatness is important, staying grounded is even more so. Even the renowned philosopher Friedrich Nietzsche reminded us of this by saying, *"One should not forget once greatness has been achieved."*

Irrespective of whether you succeed or fail, life passes quickly and soon enough everyone will disappear. For this reason, it's essential to remember that your time here on Earth should be used wisely for personal growth and the betterment of humanity as a whole. It's important to focus on making progress toward your goals, rather than dwelling on past mistakes and experiences, because before you know it, you'll cease to exist, just like everybody else.

We are all travellers on a journey destined to reach death. As we traverse the winding roads of life, it is imperative that we ponder this question: "Who am I and when will I disappear?"

Seneca often addressed this question in his writings, offering timeless advice and insight. He reminded us to prioritise our present selves over our future selves, saying, *"If you wish to be loved, love."* In other words, it is up to you in the here and now to ensure you are lovable. You must live in the moment if you are going to be remembered for who you truly are.

On a similar note, Epictetus advised against getting too caught up in what could have been. He said, *"It's not what happens to you, but how you react to it that matters."* It is not so much about what happened, or what may happen, but rather your perception of these events that makes all the difference. If you remain level-headed and stay true to yourself despite external factors, you will fade away leaving behind a legacy worth remembering.

Marcus Aurelius offered another thought-provoking perspective in saying, *"Our fate changes with time, or perhaps with changing attitudes toward life."* Here he is referring to our ability as individuals to control our destiny through attitude and perspective. We can decide how we go out into the world each day based on our outlook on life. Through conscious effort and understanding of yourself, you can channel your inner power toward leading a meaningful existence, and one that will be remembered long after you have left this world.

Although inescapable, death does not need to be something feared and dreaded. Instead, embrace the concept as an opportunity for self-reflection and improvement. As Seneca reminds us, *"Death smiles at us all but all a man can do is smile back."* This is an acknowledgment that living well is more important than living long. Each of us should take comfort from this during times of uncertainty and doubt.

Your character or how you behave in life may be your legacy after death. Practice finding peace within your own mind, stay humble, focus on your goals as your contribution to humanity, love others as you would like to be loved yourself, manage well how you react in life, and keep a positive and constructive attitude toward life to live the best life you can.

What Has Been Given Can be Taken Away

Living with the knowledge that death can take anything away at any moment is a difficult concept to come to terms with. It requires an acceptance of your own mortality and a commitment to making the most of life. Indeed, life is more precious when you take ownership of it and choose to live in a manner that recognises the importance of each day. Rather than surrendering to despair in the face of your mortality, you should strive for joy and growth.

Our lives consist mostly of temporary possessions which can vanish at any given instance due to things outside of our control. This suggests that achieving true contentment boils down to possessing those things which cannot be easily taken away from us; things such as relationships with others (friends/family) which offer much more value than material objects. Knowing this should fill us with profound gratitude for those around us.

Our sense of security is fragile as riches and health can quickly vanish. Nothing in life is permanent and it's foolish to think that our current circumstances will remain the same forever. Socrates said, *"Beware the barrenness of a busy life."* This is a reminder that pursuing your own successes without taking into account the transient nature of life is futile if all your hard work may be rendered meaningless due to changes in circumstances beyond your control. Strive to find a balance between working for success and accepting that nothing lasts forever.

Ecclesiastes reminded us to take the necessary steps to make our lives meaningful while they last: *"Do not put your trust in princes, nor in a son of man, in whom there is no help. His spirit departs, he returns to his Earth; in that very day his plans perish."* True fulfilment must come from within by living for moments mindful of their impermanence rather than expectations for the future, as they too will soon pass away.

The lesson here is simple yet powerful. Everything must end eventually and whatever has been given can be taken away just as quickly. To make our time count, we must embrace an attitude of appreciation for what we have now and not place too much faith in things outside ourselves. We have been given this brief time on Earth. Let us use it wisely, and carefully reassess our priorities before it slips through our fingers like sand.

Life is a precarious journey, and nothing is certain beyond the present moment. *"All of us have had something taken away from us at some point in life; it is nature's way of reminding us that everything we receive can also be taken away."* Seneca's words provide an important reminder that nothing can be taken for granted, and the things which we hold dear can be taken away so quickly.

The great teacher Pema Chödrön reflected this sentiment in her writing: *"One of the best ways to understand impermanence is to look around you: everything changes. Everything arises and passes away. Whether it's a feeling or an object, it appears for a while and then it goes."* With these words, she reminds us that nothing stays constant forever; whatever has been given can also be taken away.

Our mortality serves as an ultimate reminder of this concept; our lives are finite, and each day brings us closer to death. Seneca wrote: *"We are in fact running down like water spilling from a vessel with a hole in it but who will take heed? Don't you know that all nature's gifts are subject to diminution?"* Here again, we find evidence of Seneca's emphasis on the fleeting nature of life and how easily things can be lost or taken away from us.

The lesson here is twofold. Firstly, never take anything for granted in life, whether material goods or relationships. If something has been given then it may just as easily be taken away at any time. Secondly, appreciate each moment for what it offers rather than worrying about those times and moments that may have passed into history already. By actively choosing to invest in things that cannot be taken away by death, such as kindness, personal growth, learning, and generosity, you will begin to create a life worth living now and forever. In Seneca's words, *"True happiness is within reach no matter where you are."*

How Would You Spend Today If There Were No Tomorrow?

Worrying about tomorrow should never overshadow enjoying today. Seneca challenged readers on a deeper level through asking what would happen if tomorrow did not come. Such knowledge (of no tomorrow) prompts immediate appreciation of current thrills and joyous experiences available through everyday interactions and adventures.

We live each day like it is the last, never really knowing when our time on Earth will end. In Seneca's words, *"Make use of your present – it has no successor."*

Today could be our last and if tomorrow does not come, how would we spend it? Try to focus on what matters most: relationships, purposeful activities, and self-reflection. These things may help you to appreciate life's shortness and make the most of it.

Marcus Aurelius said, *"Do not act as if you had ten thousand years to throw away."* His message being we must remain aware that life is transient and make wise decisions about how to spend our time. If you fail to make use of time today, the opportunities presented to you may never return, and they will be lost forever.

Greek philosopher Diogenes once said, *"Live every day as if your life had just begun."* Each day should be embraced fully because time is so fleeting and fragile.

Reflections on this topic help us accept the limited nature of life's duration and find ways to live intentionally with conscious effort and thoughtfulness toward others.

One way of doing this is to focus on the most important aspects of life. What matters most in our lives? Are we pursuing goals that truly matter, or chasing trifles? It may be time to assess your priorities and take stock of what really matters.

Another approach is to give more time to those you love and care about, as they are often neglected in daily routines. Even a small gesture such as sending a text message can make a big difference to someone's day. *"Love many things, for therein lies the true strength, and whosoever loves much performs much, and can accomplish much, and what is done in love is done well."*

Spending some quality alone-time can help to uncover hidden potential within you. Taking just half an hour off from your busy schedule to contemplate your innermost thoughts can do wonders for your mental health. It was Aristotle who said, *"Knowing yourself is the beginning of all wisdom."*

In case tomorrow doesn't come, make today count as something special and memorable by pursuing meaningful activities instead of indulging in trivial tasks. Life is fragile, and if tomorrow doesn't come, how would you spend today? Seneca said, *"Life is short, and you do not have much time to gladden the hearts of those who travel with you. So be swift to love! Make haste to be kind!"* It's true; if tomorrow doesn't come, each passing moment becomes precious. We need to make sure that every second counts and that we are living our best lives.

"I never think of the future; it comes soon enough." This comment made by Albert Einstein is a reminder that life can end in an instant without warning. To live fully, one must embrace life while you still have time.

John Lennon also had words of wisdom to say on the topic of using today wisely: *"Life is what happens when you're busy making other plans."* It's important to prioritise your happiness over external goals or expectations. Instead of striving for something in the future which may never happen, try to find joy in the present moments that will define how you remember your life should tomorrow never come.

Throughout history, wise people have shared their advice on understanding the importance of living each day as if tomorrow may not arrive. Take heed from these timeless words and learn how to prioritise meaningful activities, appreciate every moment, appreciate your loved ones, take time to reflect, avoid wasting time fretting about the past or the future, and be thankful for what you have right now before time runs out.

Living fearlessly means embracing death without driving yourself mad wondering what happens once its inevitable occurrence has passed. Live with passion and enthusiasm for current pursuits, while simultaneously respecting limitations imposed by natural forces. This allows you to find satisfaction regardless of whether tomorrow comes. Having lived fully makes everything else irrelevant, since nothing can be taken away except physical existence itself.

What Can Death Not Take Away?

When faced with difficult moments or insurmountable obstacles, remember the words attributed to philosopher Arthur Schopenhauer: *"Death gives us sleep innumerable; why then should life be thought a burden?"* Truly embracing this idea allows you not only to cope with life's pains, but also to equip yourself to strive for greatness regardless of knowing your inevitable fate.

By choosing a lifestyle in which death can't take away what matters most – such as love or meaningful relationships – you will gain perspective on life's briefness and be better able to maximise the time given to you here on Earth.

In the words of Seneca, *"Let us prepare our minds as if we'd come to the very end of life. Let us postpone nothing.*" This quote is a reminder that life is short and fleeting, and that to make the most of it, we must choose to live in a way that means death cannot take anything away.

Living with this understanding affects how we spend our time and how we seize each day. It affects how we view wealth, possessions, legacy, and relationships. All the things that once seemed so important become irrelevant in death.

This understanding will help you focus on the most important things in life while avoiding any distractions and irrelevant pursuits. Cognitive scientist Steven Pinker added to this when he said, "*We all face the same ultimate dilemma: to tear ourselves away from sightseeing and dallying and get on with the business at hand: life itself.*"

Perhaps most importantly of all, living with an understanding of mortality refocuses our energies into something that will outlast us: a meaningful existence that benefits others, not just ourselves. This idea was a firm belief of Greek philosopher Epicurus. He wrote: "*The whole struggle of human life consists in being able to endure the present without being afraid of the future.*" In these words, he emphasises that fear of death should not paralyse us from doing what needs to be done today.

It can be a daunting thought, and may seem difficult to achieve, but it is actually quite simple. Live your best life now by avoiding distractions that take you away from what matters most; don't settle for materialism or superficial endeavours; focus on relationships; stay mindful of your mortality, and make every day count. These are things that will remain, regardless of whether you physically exist anymore.

Lessons from Death Comes Quickly

Life is a privilege. Learn now how to best use precious moments, and appreciate every experience, however small. Recognise mortality, and work intentionally toward attaining happiness.

Have courage and let go of needless worries that drain away time, mental energy, joy, and potential, while reducing capacity for meaningful actions and interactions with others.

During chaos or sorrow there will always be something to hold onto if you remain open enough to find it, so live in the present and learn to appreciate all that life offers you.

To take control of your destiny, you must recognise how fleeting life is, manage your time with self-discipline, identify and prioritise meaningful activities, break down tasks into manageable and achievable subtasks, and avoid distractions.

Have achievable goals in mind and be consistent in pursuing them. Make every day count toward self-improvement, even if you only take a small step each day. Be grateful for the things you already have, recognise your limits, and allow yourself rest and relaxation too.

Your character or how you behave in life may be your legacy after death. Practice finding peace within your own mind. Stay humble, focus on your goals as your contribution to humanity, love others as you would like to be loved yourself, manage well how you react in life, and keep a positive and constructive attitude to life to live the best life you can.

Never take anything for granted in life, whether material goods or relationships. If something has been given then it may just as easily be taken away at any time. By actively choosing to invest in things that cannot be taken away by death, such as kindness, personal growth, learning, and generosity, you will begin to create a life worth living now and forever.

Having lived fully makes everything else irrelevant, since nothing can be taken away except physical existence itself.

Live your best life now by avoiding distractions that take you away from what matters most. Don't settle for materialism or superficial endeavours; focus on relationships; stay mindful of your mortality, and make each day count.

Chapter 7

Live Your Path Freely

Zeth was always expected to do what was expected of him by his family and society. His father and mother were both occupational therapists and assumed that he would follow on in their shoes. He had done everything he was asked – gained good grades, gone to college, and even joined his parents' practice, as everyone expected him to do – but despite it all, he still felt like something was missing.

One day, Zeth had had enough and decided to make a change. He decided it was time for him to live freely and reject the expectations of others. He decided to take a leap of faith and follow his own path instead of staying firmly entrenched in the paths already laid out for him. Zeth was passionate about his art and soon enough, he realised that this was what he truly wanted to do in life. He no longer felt like he needed anyone else's approval or that he had to meet their expectations. He dedicated himself to his art and worked as a tutor, occasionally selling his work to supplement his income. His parents soon found a replacement for him in the practice and could see that he was happier. With his newfound happiness, Zeth also spent more quality time with his parents, by choice rather than through his sense of duty. His relationships with his family therefore improved too.

With his new courage and self-confidence, Zeth finally lived his life according to his own standards, not those of someone else. He was free from external expectations, and with every passing moment he felt more alive than ever before.

Accountability for Your Life

In the words of Rumi, *"Let yourself be silently drawn by the strange pull of what you really love. It will not lead you astray."*

Many of us will have felt like Zeth, especially while growing up. Seneca believed that rejecting the opinions of others was an essential element of living a responsible life and becoming the person you wish to be. He knew that taking ownership of your choices would liberate you from predetermined pathways, allowing you to forge your own path and shape your future as you want it.

Releasing yourself from total dependence on other people's viewpoints means taking full ownership over your life and accepting responsibility for each decision you make. Rejecting the opinion of another is not a sign of disrespect, but rather an acknowledgment that each individual must own their decisions and choices and be able to make their own future. In Seneca's words, *"You are a sufficient guide to yourself, if you carefully direct your own steps."*

The concept of rejecting someone's opinion has been explored by many thought leaders throughout philosophy and history. Confucius said, *"Everything has its beauty, but not everyone sees it,"* while Ralph Waldo Emerson argued that opinions should be seen as a starting point and tempered with experience when he said, *"Things are only opinions about which we may differ."*

Rejecting other people's opinions means taking responsibility for your own life. Doing so allows you the freedom to find your own way, unencumbered by others' ideas or expectations. Taking charge of your life in this way helps you to create more meaningful experiences, free from outside influences. You can then focus on making decisions based on your values and aspirations, rather than simply accepting what others suggest without question.

Actively resist the status quo and look beyond the frames presented by others. Ask hard questions about the world around you and plot a course that puts your values first. In this way, you will craft a life defined by meaning instead of one which conforms to what somebody else believes is right or wrong.

Power of Choice

With this power of choice comes a sense of empowerment; an understanding that your future lies in your hands. You must break free from the chains of expectations, ignoring what society tells you is right or wrong and instead explore for yourself who you really want to be and how you want to live. Seneca speaks of this "power of choice" in his writings, noting its great potential for both freedom and growth. He wrote: *"It is our choices that show us what we truly are far more than our abilities."*

The power of choice is a concept that has been discussed and celebrated for millennia, but it is only recently that we've begun to take the idea more seriously. Seneca, in his On Providence paper wrote: *"The very thought of freedom from fear is enough to fill us with joy and gratitude."* In other words, taking control of your life path gives you a sense of optimism about being able to guide your own future, something for which you can be truly thankful.

"It never ceased to amaze me: we all love ourselves more than other people but care more about their opinions than our own." These words were written by Marcus Aurelius in AD180, and he makes the point that our real power lies within ourselves. We must not allow others to dictate our life choices or give you false hope, we must take charge and live freely without constraints.

It's true that few of us have the capacity or even the desire to be completely autonomous beings, but countless teachers, leaders, and philosophers throughout history have pointed to one thing: ultimately, all of us – each and every human being – has sole responsibility for their own choices.

In modern times, this ancient truth is echoed by many well-known thinkers. For example, Oprah Winfrey said, *"If you want your life to be a magnificent story then begin by realising that you are the author and every day you have the opportunity to write a new page."* She reminds us that the power always rests in our hands, and it's up to us how we design our stories and share them with those around us.

Although some may feel overwhelmed by such responsibility – after all none of us is perfect – taking control of your life helps build mental fortitude and strength. Each decision made conscientiously takes patience and persistence, and when faced with daunting tasks or overwhelming odds, it becomes easier over time to stand firm in these moments of uncertainty.

The concept that choices greatly influence how much time matters or doesn't matter in any given person's life path ties into this idea perfectly. Making genuine decisions rooted in reason rather than impulse helps ensure long-term success regardless of what kind of goal an individual may choose to pursue.

Seneca once said, *"To live happily is an inward power which depends entirely upon ourselves."* The power of choice is indeed an internal one; an ability, if developed correctly, that allows anyone to live authentically, productively, and happily despite external circumstances.

Oprah Winfrey also said, *"Your true identity is not meant to be hidden or suppressed, rather, it is meant to be expressed in your unique way."* Her message in these words is that individuals should not only to take charge of their paths, but also embrace who they are in the process; something that requires bravery but will pay off in self-confidence.

By understanding both where you have come from as well as where you want to go, you can leverage the power of choice to take ownership over your life without feeling like a victim at the mercy of others or outside forces. This combination creates a sense of strength, even if external circumstances remain unchanged; an inner strength that radiates outward into other aspects of life including relationships, work life or academic pursuits, and even community engagement projects.

It is important for us all to remember that having autonomy over ourselves does not absolve us from responsibility for our actions or lack thereof. It merely serves as a foundation upon which lasting success can be built with patience and dedication over time. Making conscious choices can help to create unique stories along your life path. By actively choosing a path in life, you can recognise the value of every moment and ensure your decisions bring you closer to achieving your goals. Break free from the chains of expectation by ignoring what society tells you is right or wrong. Choose instead to explore for yourself who you really want to be and how you want to live.

Freedom as an Intentional Priority

To truly break away from external opinions and pressures, freedom must become an intentional priority in life. This involves making conscious decisions about how you will spend your time, (for example, pursuing activities that bring joy or connecting with people that honour your true interests and values) to guard your autonomy against external forces.

Life is short, and yet so much of the time we live as if it is infinite. We struggle to find a balance between work and play, and between material comforts and deeper connection with ourselves and others. But, what happens when we embrace our mortality and make freedom an intentional priority?

Seneca advocated a life of convenience in contrast to one of luxury. In Moral Letters to Lucilius, he wrote: *"It is the sign of a great mind to dislike greatness; and before you can understand that thought, you must rid yourself of all your possessions, for how can anyone think liberty worth having unless he has tasted slavery?"*

By discarding our attachment to material things and engaging with life more deeply, we open ourselves up to true freedom and meaning. Philosopher Alan Watts also promoted this belief, saying, *"The only way to make sense out of change is to plunge into it, move with it, and join the dance."*

At first glance this may seem like an impossible feat because life can be complicated, unpredictable, and full of difficult decisions. But, by committing ourselves to living freely – acknowledging death as inevitable but not treating it as a punishment – we open up our lives to exploration and growth, and every single moment becomes precious because it may not come again.

It's important to go beyond just thinking about opportunities for freedom. We must actively choose them. Freedom starts with the willingness to give up something of who you are now to make way for something new that wants to emerge in your life. Freedom always requires giving up something secure in exchange for something unknown but free.

Living freely means making such sacrifices consciously, rather than waiting until circumstances force us into doing what we don't want. It means being brave enough to follow your own path – even when it looks uncertain or frightening – because ultimately it leads you closer to fulfilment. *"There are many kinds of freedoms, but some are harder won than others."* With these words, poet Mary Oliver reminds us that living freely means embracing paths less obvious because they bring greater rewards on your journey through life. These are rewards that cannot be bought or taken away from you because they originate from within yourself.

There are many different kinds of freedom, some more attainable than others. The freedom to choose what you do with your time and energy is an example of a tangible freedom; the ability to make decisions about how you spend your days and who you spend them with. Other forms of freedom can be harder to acquire, such as emotional or spiritual freedom, and the liberation from fear and anxiety that comes from trusting yourself and finding meaning in life. Financial freedom is also an important form of autonomy, relieving the pressure of needing a steady income or worrying about debts or investments. Beyond these, educational freedoms are essential for learning new skills and expanding your knowledge base. Political freedom is fundamental for creating a just society where everyone's rights are respected and protected.

Intangible freedom also extends to being free from judgment or unrealistic standards placed upon you by yourself or others. In essence, intangible freedom is more complex and powerful than tangible freedom because it requires looking beneath the surface of the

ROBERT N. JACOBS

physical world to identify and address deeper needs for autonomy, respect, and self-determination.

We all experience moments of uncertainty and insecurity throughout our lives, but it's important to learn how to move past any feelings of inadequacy. Doing so requires self-compassion, trusting your instincts, taking risks, and being open to new experiences, allowing you to break free from the limiting beliefs that keep you from achieving your true potential. It's breaking free that gives you the confidence and strength to pursue your passions and live life on your own terms.

Examples of self-compassion techniques include:

1. Acknowledging and honouring your emotions without judgment.
2. Practicing mindfulness and being fully aware of the present moment.
3. Taking regular breaks from negative thoughts and limiting beliefs.
4. Speaking kindly to yourself, accepting mistakes as a part of life's journey, and treating yourself with the same love and respect you would give to a close friend or family member.
5. Treating setbacks as learning opportunities rather than personal failures.
6. Surrounding yourself with supportive people who understand and honour your worth despite any challenges you may face in life.

In summary, freedom must become an intentional priority in life. By discarding attachment to material things and engaging with life more deeply, you will open yourself up to true freedom. Living freely means being brave enough to follow your own path – even when it looks uncertain or frightening – because ultimately it leads you closer to fulfilment. It means practicing self-compassion, trusting your instincts, taking risks, and being open to new experiences.

Free Yourself from Others' Expectations

It is often difficult to resist the outside pressures of society or family and their expectations. As individuals, we often struggle to evade conformity or to reject outside expectations, particularly if such decisions become intertwined with our sense of identity.

Seneca said, *"It is the power of the mind to be unconquerable."* An important step in building autonomy is unburdening yourself from others' expectations. Those others might be family members or friends who may unknowingly be influencing your choices by setting predetermined boundaries around what constitutes success or failure in your life. Releasing these narrow constraints opens up immense possibilities, while also protecting your autonomy over personal decisions in life.

The key is to find a way of unburdening yourself from other people's expectations. You must learn how to establish your own boundaries and appreciate your personal definitions of success. American painter Thomas Hart Benton once said, *"Life should be judged according to one's own standards, not someone else's."* Rather than setting unrealistic goals based on what you think others want from you, focus instead on what *you* value most and establish an achievable road map for getting there.

Life coach Karen Salmansohn made a good point when she said, *"Actions speak louder than genetics."* The message in her words is that it is not our genes or family background that determine our success in life, but our actions, the choices we make, and how we spend our time. It is possible to create a positive impact on your life despite negative family dynamics by making conscious decisions to put effort into bettering yourself and striving toward better outcomes in the future. You must actively choose to reject external expectations and resist conforming to live life with meaning and authenticity.

For inspiration on how to do this, we can look toward famous thought leaders who have spoken at length on their own experiences. Stephen Covey suggests beginning with the end in mind. He says, *"Visualise what you want in the long term so you can utilise your immediate choices as steps toward getting there."* In this way, long-term goal setting allows greater control over your actions and decision-making so that you may achieve balance between external expectations and internal autonomy.

A great first step is to reflect on your values and goals. By doing this, you can recognise what is truly important to you rather than what society feels you should be striving for or worrying about. Once your own personal values have been determined, you can strive to live by them without being hindered by external pressures. Then, establish clear goals and objectives as part of your daily routine. By becoming actively engaged in managing your life in this way, rather than allowing yourself to become consumed by societal expectations, you can move toward achieving true self-realisation and satisfaction.

The art of unburdening yourself can provide invaluable relief in areas where you feel confined or oppressed by outside forces. It allows you to focus solely on your own needs and desires and make decisions based only on your personal values, instead of catering to external pressures imposed on you by society or individuals close to you.

In addition to establishing your own values, another key step in unburdening yourself from others' expectations involves setting clear boundaries with those around you. It is important to communicate respectfully yet firmly when expressing your needs or desires, thereby making sure those around you are aware of what you are most comfortable with.

Taking time out for relaxation is important if we are to avoid feeling overwhelmed. Find solace in looking inwardly at yourself, as this will (in time) allow you to reject external pressures. If you manage to maintain this sense of self-awareness throughout your daily life then you may be able to resist societal norms, and avoid any accompanying feelings of anxiety or fear.

Practice self-compassion and talk kindly to yourself when things don't go according to plan. Learn how to forgive yourself when necessary and take it easy on yourself while still working toward your goals. In this way, you will have accomplished something truly remarkable: you will have liberated yourself from crippling external pressures, and you will be able to embrace a life of purposeful freedom.

Cultivating an environment of self-forgiveness devoid of harshness and judgment can help to relieve pressure regarding failure or making mistakes. Philosopher Friedrich Nietzsche once said, *"You must have chaos within you to give birth to a dancing star."* These words encapsulate the notion that mistakes should be embraced as part of an individual's journey toward self-actualisation and emancipation from restrictive societal norms.

By understanding that failure is inevitable, you can begin taking necessary steps toward liberating yourself from external pressures while also staying true to your internal values and ethics. This paves the way for fulfilling life experiences rooted in personal growth and creative exploration.

Be the change you wish to see in the world by liberating yourself from outside expectations and embracing your own values, mistakes, and autonomy. Strive for *the power of the mind to be unconquerable.*

Actively choose to reject external expectations and resist conforming. In this way, you will live life with meaning and authenticity. Be a fully coherent and individualistic version of yourself, unmarred by society's domineering hand.

Useless Comparisons

Seneca warned of the fruitlessness of comparing yourself to others. This does nothing but lead you down impossible paths with unrealistic aspirations. No two people are equal. Each individual has his/her own strengths and weaknesses, which makes comparison useless, serving only to generate envy.

"It is quite sad and misguided for a person to put their trust in public opinion." Seneca followed these words with, *"Those who follow it are driven by empty vanity, and those who criticise it live in pain and jealousy. This is why comparison should be avoided at all costs."*

In his book, Walden, Henry David Thoreau also discouraged comparisons with others. He warned against making judgments about your worthiness based on external standards set by what he called the "mass of men." Comparisons with others have been used throughout history as a way to measure personal status or rank within a society, but these often result in shallow judgments as you cannot see another person's true potential – or potential success or failure. Instead of measuring your worth against someone else's achievements, time should be devoted to focusing on your own competence levels and capabilities so that you can reach your potential regardless of what anyone else is doing.

Comparing yourself to others can lead to reduced self-esteem. Thinking that other people are more capable or successful than you can cause you to feel inadequate and less confident about your strengths and abilities. On the flip side, comparing ourselves favourably to others can turn into arrogance or unhealthy competition that can be just as damaging in the long run.

French philosopher Blaise Pascal summed this idea up neatly when he said, *"Comparisons are odious."* Comparing your life to someone else's life serves no purpose as you cannot possibly know what they have gone through, nor can you realistically compete against them if they have already achieved success while following a different path to your own. As Henry David Thoreau famously put it, *"If a man does not keep pace with his companions, perhaps it is because he hears a different drummer. Let him step to the music which he hears, however measured or far away."*

Your self-worth should not be measured by external standards, but by your own capabilities and how you decide to use them. By setting realistic goals based on your individual talents and interests, you can focus on developing *your* skills and talents so that you can reach your full potential. Additionally, learning to appreciate your own accomplishments and successes is important for fostering healthy self-esteem. You should strive to achieve a balanced lifestyle that allows you enough time to invest in your goals while also providing enough time for relaxation and leisure activities to ensure that you remain content with yourself and the progress you are making.

Comparing yourself with others will only lead to unrealistic aspirations because everyone is unique. Thinking others are more successful will make you feel inadequate, and thinking they are less successful may lead to becoming arrogant. Focus instead on your own competence levels and aim to reach your own potential.

Adversity as Opportunity for Growth

Rejecting other's opinions can initially be overwhelming, and progress may feel less certain without external guidance. Nevertheless, adversity should be thoughtfully considered as an opportunity for growth, since embracing uncertainty helps stimulate creative problem-solving skills, leading to greater self-trust. This self-trust is necessary when forging new pathways independent from external narrations.

Adversity is not without its uses: it can make a man wiser if he meets it in the right spirit. This sentiment rings true for those who recognise adversity as an opportunity for growth. Though life's challenges can feel insurmountable at times, these struggles can also act as beacons of light, bestowing upon us wisdom and strength to make life better.

Steve Jobs once said, *"Sometimes life hits you in the head with a brick. Don't lose faith. I'm convinced that the only thing that kept me going was that I loved what I did. You've got to find what you love."* Adversity may open the door to new opportunities, and to greater growth and development that will help to create a better future.

Keep in mind that a journey of a thousand miles begins with a single step. Taking just one small action, despite any obstacles, demonstrates immense courage and resilience, both qualities integral to fighting off adversity and turning it to your advantage. Having the courage to continue despite challenges allows you to re-imagine your negative experiences as valuable lessons learned for personal growth and advancement.

Marcus Aurelius wrote: *"The impediment to action advances action. What stands in the way becomes the way."* Any hardship can be used as leverage for both inner transformation and success. Never forget that you have the power within yourself to overcome difficulty through creative solutions; each obstacle presents a chance to step forward rather than backward.

Seneca encouraged us to look at adversities as an opportunity for growth and strength. He believed that to develop fully, you must embrace hardships and use them as a platform to gain greater understanding and appreciation. *"Difficulties strengthen the mind, as labour does the body."*

Perceiving adversity as an opportunity for growth is a timeless message proposed by many influential figures throughout history, reminding us of the courage necessary for personal development. It's clear that only through embracing challenging situations can we truly grow into our fullest self and find purpose in the journey of life.

Victor Frankl, psychiatrist and Holocaust survivor said, *"When we are no longer able to change a situation, we are challenged to change ourselves."* He believed that even when faced with tremendous difficulty or suffering, we should strive to control how we respond. This was also the belief of Mahatma Gandhi when he said, *"Strength does not come from physical capacity. It comes from an indomitable will."* With these words, he emphasised the powerful influence of attitude when dealing with difficulties and tribulations.

Other notable figures have left a legacy of quotes that add weight to this sentiment. Theodore Roosevelt said, *"Believe you can and you're halfway there."* Winston Churchill gave a famous speech in which he said, *"Never give in – never, never, never, never…"* and Vince Lombardi wisely stated, *"It's not whether you get knocked down; it's whether you get up."*

Perceiving adversity as an opportunity for growth requires a conscious effort on your part. When you look beyond challenging circumstances, even if just for one moment, you may register possibilities of success or personal evolution that were previously unavailable or unseen.

Embrace Complexity

We often feel drawn toward the familiar, the tried-and-true paths that history has told us have been successful in navigating life's journey. It can be tempting to define yourself rigidly by following those secure and now apparently simple footsteps.

However, life's most rewarding experiences come when you are willing to take risks and embrace unpredictability. Oversimplification only serves to limit potential for growth and development; it does not allow for meaningful dialogue between different perspectives or values. A person who clings too strongly to their view of what should be misses out on opportunities for creative problem-solving and understanding. By embracing ambiguity and complexity, you open yourself up to a world full of possibilities that can transform your outlook on everyday matters, as well as major issues such as politics, social dynamics, and philosophy.

To make sense of any given situation, we need to draw upon multiple sources of knowledge and viewpoints. We cannot rely simply on personal experience or preconceived ideas if we want to get an accurate picture of the world around us. Learning how to navigate the ever-changing landscape with assurance requires practice and dedication, much like attempting a new type of art or mastering a new language. Success comes with consistent effort over time, rather than instantaneous comprehension. By remaining open-minded despite uncertainty, however difficult this may be at times, you will win the potential for immense understanding beyond what you had previously thought was possible.

Seneca captures the concept of avoiding oversimplification and embracing ambiguity and complexity in his writings. In life, we may feel like all the winds of fortune are blowing against us, but that is only true if we do not have a clear vision for our lives. When we try to simplify matters or overlook complexities to arrive at solutions quickly, we risk missing out on crucial details and making mistakes. In his book, Long Walk to Freedom, Nelson Mandela said, *"Do not judge me by my successes, judge me by how many times I fell down and got back up again."* By focusing on the idea of success without accounting for potential mistakes along the way, you can easily forget what makes success meaningful: the strength it takes to continue in the face of multiple setbacks.

Complexity offers us valuable insights into the world around us instead of flattening our understanding of it. We can look beyond superficial observations and discover deeper connections and patterns that would otherwise remain hidden if we were too quick to draw conclusions based on shallow logic. By recognising complexity, rather than trying to reduce it, we empower ourselves with an ability to shape our own destinies instead of waiting for them to unfold passively before us.

In conclusion, avoid oversimplification and acknowledge the ambiguity and complexity in life. Look beyond the surface-level observations and discover deeper connections between different ideas or viewpoints to gain a richer understanding. Moreover, when trying to make sense of your life or any kind of situation in general, consciously accept different viewpoints simultaneously. Take time to acknowledge ambiguity and complexity and to gain valuable insights about your own true nature and diversity at large.

Self-Reliance in Decision-Making

Making wise choices can often feel intimidating because of the high degree of permanence. However, no decision has only one outcome. In fact, according to The Alchemist author Paulo Coelho, *"There is only one thing that makes a dream impossible to achieve: the fear of failure."* The choice between opting for safety or taking risks can be daunting, but each relies heavily on self-esteem and self-worth; two concepts deeply rooted in personal development that cannot be taken away by external forces.

Whether you are choosing which path to take or which values to advocate, practicing self-reliance means trusting in your own intuition. Eleanor Roosevelt, political figure, diplomat, activist, and first lady of the United States from 1933 to 1945 said, *"You must do the thing you think you cannot do."* This requires recognising that your fate lies within your own hands. However, you need to acknowledge the importance of financial stability when making decisions that align with your deepest desires and intentions, as such choices may impact on your life later.

When you take a step back to pause and consider your decisions, you may find greater clarity, and perhaps come to a conclusion that is based on what is best for you, rather than one based on emotions or someone else's opinion.

Self-reliance allows you to tap into your inner strength and employ it as a tool when making decisions that will affect your life. It also allows you to shape your own destiny instead of relying on someone else's opinion or advice. To practice self-reliance, you must first rid yourself of any negative thoughts or attitudes that might be preventing you from believing in yourself. You must be willing to take risks, even if you are unsure about the outcome, because this is how real growth begins.

As Henry David Thoreau once said, *"I learned this, at least, by my experiment: that if one advances confidently in the direction of his dreams, and endeavours to live the life which he has imagined, he will meet with a success unexpected in common hours."* Confidence is key when practicing self-reliance. Believe in yourself and you will see results!

Self-reliance means being patient with your thought processes and understanding that it takes time to arrive at meaningful conclusions. However, taking ownership of decisions makes them more powerful.

"Very little is needed to make a happy life; it is all within yourself in your way of thinking." These words of wisdom come from Meditations, authored by Marcus Aurelius in 180AD, and they remind us of the power we hold within. Practicing self-reliance helps us remain mindful of what truly matters and guides us toward living an authentic life – one filled with joy, satisfaction, peace, and contentment. When we are true to our values and place emphasis on them during decision-making, this journey called life becomes easier and much more fulfilling.

Self-reliance helps you make decisions without fear or worry because you know your decisions are based on what you feel is best for yourself – no one else but yourself. So, keep calm and practice self-reliance!

Practicing self-reliance can come in many forms, but some of the most impactful and common ways include:

- Questioning yourself – don't be afraid to ask yourself questions like, "Does this decision align with my values?" or, "What are the consequences of this decision?" or, "What do I truly want?"

- Taking ownership – own your decisions and be accountable for them. This means not relying on other people's opinions or advice when making important choices.
- Overcoming fear – fear is one of the main obstacles that prevents us from practicing self-reliance. Courageously stepping out of your comfort zone will help you grow as an individual.
- Employing mindfulness – being mindful allows you to slow down and really assess a situation before taking action. This helps to ensure decisions are based on what is best for you, rather than making knee-jerk responses to external pressures.

In summary, trust in your own intuition, recognise that your fate lies in your own hands, and apply your self-reliance to shape your own destiny. Question what you really want, take ownership of your decisions, put fear aside, dare to step out of your comfort zone, and take time to reflect on your decisions.

Courage from Active Reflection

Courage can be developed through active reflection. By pausing and reflecting on your life, you become more open to the courage necessary to conquer your fears and rise above your challenges.

To draw from the legacy of other thought leaders, William Blake once said, *"Where reason can refute presumption, let presumption yield to reason."*

This reinforces a belief held by Seneca, namely that it is only through actively engaging with fear, and by questioning its validity instead of retreating from it, that you can begin to strengthen your courage.

Ralph Waldo Emerson pointed out that growth is never fast-forwarded by comfort or convenience when he said, *"Our strength grows out of our weakness."* With these words, he is suggesting that stepping outside of your comfort zone leads to increased levels of personal fortitude. Reflection gives us the chance to actively consider our weaknesses and embrace them as tools for growth and development.

The power of self-reflection for developing courage has been well documented throughout history, inviting us all to take a step back and consider what is truly necessary for making progress in life. In doing so, we create new opportunities for ourselves and move closer toward true liberation, all while reflecting deeply on what makes us who we are today.

As Mark Twain said, *"Courage is resistance to fear, mastery of fear – not absence of fear."* The idea that we should have no fear and be completely fearless is false; what matters is having the courage to take the necessary steps despite fears or doubts. To have courage, you need to confront fears head on by actively reflecting on past experiences and understanding why a particular outcome was achieved or failed.

Active reflection helps you research why something didn't work as expected and what might be done differently next time. It pushes you to think beyond your comfort zone while also helping build confidence in yourself, confidence that can help give clarity when facing difficult decisions in life. Regular practice of active reflection provides opportunities for self-improvement, which in turn leads to genuine courage over time.

Oscar Wilde once said, *"Man can believe the impossible, but man can never believe the improbable."* To build courage, you need to believe in the impossible. Believe that you can push yourself further than before without being afraid of failure or success, simply allowing yourself to experience growth objectively without judging results too harshly. Active reflection provides a platform for such growth by causing us to reflect deeply on past experiences so that mistakes are avoided again in future situations, and lessons for improvement are learned.

Building courage through active reflection provides us with an opportunity for steady development by enabling us to learn from both failures and successes and move forward every day with more wisdom than before.

Lessons from Live Your Path Freely

Focus on making decisions based on your values and aspirations, rather than simply accepting what others suggest without question.

Remember that having autonomy does not absolve you from responsibility, but serves as a foundation upon which lasting success can be built with patience and dedication.

Freedom must become an intentional priority in life. Living freely means being brave enough to follow your own path – even when it looks uncertain or frightening – because ultimately it leads you closer to fulfilment. It means practicing self-compassion, trusting your instincts, taking risks, and being open to new experiences.

Actively choose to reject external expectations and resist conforming. In this way, you will live life with meaning and authenticity. Be a fully coherent and individualistic version of yourself, unmarred by society's domineering hand.

Comparing yourself to others will lead to unrealistic aspirations because everyone is unique. Thinking others are more successful will make you feel inadequate, and thinking they are less successful may lead to becoming arrogant. Focus instead on your own competence levels and aim to reach your own potential.

Perceiving adversity as an opportunity for growth requires a conscious effort on your part. When you look beyond challenging circumstances, you may register possibilities of success or personal evolution that were previously unavailable or unseen.

Avoid oversimplification and acknowledge the ambiguity and complexity in life. Accept different viewpoints simultaneously, take time to acknowledge ambiguity and complexity, and to gain valuable insights about your own true nature and diversity at large.

Trust in your own intuition, recognise that your fate lies in your own hands, and apply your self-reliance to shape your own destiny.

Question what you really want, take ownership of your decisions, put fear aside, dare to step out of your comfort zone, and take time to reflect on your decisions.

Build courage through active reflection. This will provide you with the opportunity for steady development by enabling you to learn from failures and successes, and move forward every day with more wisdom than before.

Chapter 8

Finding Contentment
with Simplicity

Once upon a time, there was a man called Max who could never find peace and contentment in his life. Max worked hard at his job, had plenty of money and possessions, but he still felt lost and unfulfilled.

He tried various distractions to fill the void inside him, but nothing seemed to work for very long. He tried going on exotic trips, buying expensive cars and clothes, even throwing himself into extreme sports, yet afterwards, he always found himself feeling just as empty as before.

One day, after all his attempts had failed, Max decided to take a risk and try something completely different; he began to simplify his life. He let go of all the excess possessions that no longer served him and he stopped worrying about impressing others with material things.

With this newfound peace of mind, Max devoted more time to the things that truly mattered. These were his family and friends, who provided unconditional love; meaningful activities such as reading books or playing music; and finding joy in small creative projects like painting or woodwork.

By reconnecting with these simpler activities in life, Max finally found what he had been searching for all along: true peace and contentment within himself.

Befriending the Impermanence of Life

Life is fleeting. In Seneca's words, *"Nothing is more active than time, and nothing has less respect for what happens to one."* This sentiment may sound bleak, but befriending the impermanence of life can yield much satisfaction and meaning in life. Recognising that time is limited is powerful, allowing us to make conscious choices about how we spend it, and providing an impetus for taking actions that we deem worthy.

Though it requires courage to accept the transience of life, this insight brings great wisdom and rewards. Buddha taught that attachment to material things, ideas, people, or emotions causes suffering. Understanding our temporal existence, on the other hand, helps us to cultivate a healthy attitude toward our interactions with them.

Recognising that life is finite encourages living fully in the present moment. Focusing on each present moment is a valuable part of befriending impermanence; it allows true gratitude for what is here now rather than attachment to what has gone or may never come. By cultivating this idea of savouring each moment before it passes, we become comfortable with change, making space for new possibilities or opportunities instead of lamenting those which are no more.

In addition to allowing us greater presence in life's moments, embracing the impermanence of life creates a sense of purpose. We become motivated, not by wanting what we don't have, but by doing something meaningful that leaves a lasting impact beyond our own lives.

Befriending impermanence invites us into a deeper relationship with ourselves, one that increases self-knowledge and understanding within a larger context, allowing us to acknowledge both times when our actions were effective and when they weren't. It helps us recognise when we should pause and when we need to take up arms, thereby granting us access to a new realm of personal growth filled with peace and innovation.

It can be extremely difficult to confront such a large philosophical concept as impermanence – as many philosophers have acknowledged – yet it offers great rewards. Confucius taught that personal growth requires reflection on one's past experiences; confronting and accepting that even these will eventually be gone creates an impetus for taking action now which will persist longer than us alone.

Recognising temporal existence creates purpose in life because it motivates us to make conscious choices about how we spend our time and take action that we deem worthy. It encourages us to live fully in the present moment, rather than regretting the past or worrying about the future, and to make the most of each fleeting moment with gratitude and contentment. By understanding our impermanence, we are better able to act out of a desire for creating something meaningful that will last beyond ourselves, which imbues a sense of purpose that is both rewarding and fulfilling.

Creating something meaningful that will outlast ourselves involves recognising our impermanence and taking thoughtful action in accordance with our convictions.

This could mean coming up with creative ideas to pursue, investing our energy and resources into meaningful projects, and devoting time to building relationships and creating positive experiences for others. It may also include actively engaging in service or volunteer work that benefits a cause we care about, writing or sharing stories that have lasting impact, or leaving an inheritance to help generations beyond us. The possibilities are endless! Ultimately, by focusing on tangible contributions that transcend us, we can strive to create something of lasting value as a legacy.

Accepting that life is limited in time provides the impetus to use it wisely, live in the moment, have a deeper relationship with your inner self, and to do something meaningful that will leave a lasting legacy beyond your own existence.

Detaching from Things

We often find ourselves attached to objects, whether they are material possessions or sentimental items, but as in Max's case, it is important to recognise that these attachments cannot bring us lasting peace and contentment. In striving for a simpler lifestyle, we must learn to appreciate these items from a distance and let go when necessary.

Much of our materialistic modern society revolves around a thirst for acquiring more and more possessions. For this reason, it is increasingly important for us to recognise the need to let go of things, both in terms of physical possessions and mental preoccupations.

This need was eloquently put into words by Henry David Thoreau when he said, *"A man is rich in proportion to the number of things he can afford to let alone."*

Epicurus believed that understanding our mortality leads to pleasure. He said, *"Death does not concern us, because as long as we exist, death is not here. And when it does come, we no longer exist."* We must break free from the desire for fame or material wealth – things that will evaporate with our own existence – and focus instead on things that bring lasting joy. These things may include spending time with friends and family, learning new skills, helping others, and being kind to ourselves.

"We are brought down by our longing for riches; we are lifted up by enriching our inner life." Spoken by Seneca, these words serve as a reminder that as much as you may cling on to material distractions, they cannot fulfil you in the way that understanding yourself can. It is precisely through this understanding that you will gain clarity on the human condition and begin to understand what really matters in life. You must relinquish your attachment to things to appreciate their importance in your life. As Epicurus noted, *"We should look upon all external goods with suspicion and realise that we do not need them if we want true happiness."*

Detaching from material things means accepting the fact that life will never be perfect; there will always be something outside our reach that tempts us with its false allure of fulfilment. Our journey toward contentment begins when we accept this truth about reality and learn to appreciate the good moments in life without

ROBERT N. JACOBS

constantly craving more, focusing instead on finding satisfaction and joy within ourselves. In the words of Marcus Aurelius, *"Very little is needed to make a happy life; it is all within yourself, in your way of thinking."* Embracing detachment allows you to refocus your attention away from external objects, helping to lead you toward internal peace and prosperity.

Seneca wrote: *"True happiness is to enjoy the present, without anxious dependence upon the future."* At its core, embracing detachment from things comes down to accepting that life is short and uncertain, and that our happiness and wellbeing need not be dependent on material possessions or accumulations of wealth. Indeed, by releasing ourselves from such attachments, we can find more joy in the intangible aspects of life – enjoying a moment with loved ones over an intimate conversation or simply experiencing the beautiful world around us.

Eagerness to acquire more tends to cloud judgment and can distract us from our true purpose in life. Buddha advised us to, *"Live each day as if your life had just begun."* By living in the moment and letting go of expectations for future outcomes and material gain, we are free to appreciate all aspects of life equally with no preferences for any one particular thing.

Letting go means recognising that accumulation of wealth or possessions alone cannot bring us lasting satisfaction. It is only when we embrace detachment from these distractions that we can begin facing reality with clear eyes, accepting what has already happened in the past instead of mourning over its unchangeable nature, or worrying about possible events in the future that may never actually happen.

Embracing detachment from things can have a profound effect on your overall wellbeing and mental health. By releasing yourself from attachment to material possessions or wealth, you will become free to appreciate the present moment without allowing past experience or future expectations to define your current state of mind. With this sense of freedom comes an enhanced appreciation of life as a whole, allowing you to recognise the importance of relationships, meaningful conversations, moments of joy, and other intangible elements that make up your life. Ultimately, embracing detachment is an exercise in liberation that allows you to pursue a simpler lifestyle filled with greater contentment and serenity than ever before.

Rejecting False Hopes and Appearances

It is easy to be taken in by false hopes and appearances; the veneer of a more pleasant world can be alluring. But, as Seneca once said, *"Nothing is more unreliable than appearances; they often lead us astray."* The truth of life is that we are born, we live briefly, and then we die. Rejecting false hopes and appearances is a vital part of understanding the shortness and finality of life.

Simplicity is a key tenet for those who wish to reject false hopes and appearances. In Seneca's words, *"The greatest abundance specifies the most diligent thrift, and it is possible to manage with a very small number of things, if one only knows which are the most important."*

Unnecessary materialistic pursuits only add more noise to our lives and distract us from what truly matters.

Philosopher Montaigne argued that people often get stuck on believing in societal norms rather than in their own authentic vision. He said, *"Let us not be led astray, by the common mistake of making a show of simplicity when in fact we are really indulging in luxury."* We must learn to take pleasure from the simple things in life instead of filling our lives with superfluous demands that don't bring us joy.

Furthermore, we shouldn't become too attached to certain goals or life outcomes, as this can create a mental "illusion of control" that leads us away from living a meaningful existence. Instead, let go of your expectations and trust that life's path will reveal itself when the time is right. The illusion of control is believing that we can control outcomes in life, even when this is not possible. This belief often leads to unhappiness and frustration if our expectations do not come to fruition. People who are stuck in this mindset believe that they have a certain level of control over aspects of their lives that are outside their control, such as other people's opinions of them.

The only way to break free from this type of thinking is to accept life's uncertainty and focus on what we can control: our attitude, behaviour, and actions. Accept that you don't have complete control and instead focus on understanding yourself deeply and living authentically without expecting too much from the world.

Happiness can be cultivated when faced with difficulty by recognising that life is full of ups and downs. It's important to approach challenges with a growth mindset, believing them to be learning opportunities. Rather than dwelling on the negative aspects of hardship, try to focus on what can be gained from the experience.

Practice self-compassion and remember that it's okay to take things one step at a time. Make time for meaningful activities such as reading, exercising, or simply spending time in nature. Cultivating resilience will help you manage difficult situations more effectively, and lead to greater happiness. Lastly, don't forget to take care of yourself. Find joy in simple pleasures like cooking your favourite meal or watching your favourite show; these simple moments can help restore balance and make any situation more manageable.

In summary, rejecting false hopes and appearances is a vital part of understanding the shortness of life. Unnecessary materialistic pursuits distract us from what truly matters. Accept life's uncertainty and focus on what you can control: your attitude, behaviour, and actions. Focus on what can be gained from hardships, and practice self-compassion.

Living with Simplicity and Gratitude

Rather than wishing for more, simplicity encourages us to be thankful for what we already have. This helps us reflect on how much potential there is in even the simplest experiences if we are willing to appreciate them fully instead of searching endlessly for something better.

Living gratefully with what we have is a beautiful yet challenging practice. As Seneca said, *"It is not one's own possessions, but the freedom of not wanting that produces happiness."* This notion of living very deeply with gratefulness for our current circumstances can be hard to commit to in an increasingly materialistic world.

Dolly Parton once said, *"The way I see it, if you want the rainbow, you gotta put up with the rain."* To make the most of life, we must learn how to savour both good times and bad times alike. True appreciation comes from understanding the value of each experience transcendently, rather than through a self-centred lens.

Although worlds apart, we learn from both Seneca and Dolly Parton that living gratefully does not mean simply enduring unhappy circumstances. Instead, it means seeking beauty and free spirit in every moment regardless of its circumstances. When you recognise your place within the universe as part of its perfection, then all moments become reminders that gratitude is always close by. Rather than engaging with feelings of deficiency or loss, practicing gratitude can help bring forth creativity and expand your compassion toward yourself and others.

Living with simplicity and gratefulness requires a willingness to be content with what we have. In Seneca's words, *"Contentment is the greatest wealth."* When you search for gratification outside your current circumstances, your search for fulfilment will seem never-ending. On the other hand, when you embrace contentment with what you have, life becomes simpler and more meaningful.

Ralph Waldo Emerson captured this idea perfectly when he said, *"He who is not contented with what he has, would not be contented with what he would like to have."* Contentment does not require giving up your dreams or passions, it helps you let go of striving only for material success. Instead, you can savour every moment as it comes.

Living gratefully also means being mindful in your daily life. Eckhart Tolle taught us that instead of ruminating over the past or worrying about the future, we should live mindfully in the present, and experience each moment fully without judgment or expectation. Doing so allows for patience and generosity toward others as well as ourselves, resulting in a deeper connection with ourselves and those around us regardless of circumstance.

Practicing gratitude by taking time out of our day to say thank you for life's simple joys, such as a beautiful sunset, a good cup of coffee, or a hug from a child, can also help us reconnect with what is truly important. Learning to accept ourselves and others unconditionally can bring us closer to understanding that we are enough just as we are.

In summary, living gratefully brings forth the understanding that there will always be enough, both inside and outside of ourselves, if we take time to appreciate it all deeply enough. All that's required to find true peace and joy within our lives is acceptance of where we are right now, no matter how much or how little we possess.

Short- and Long-Term Contentment

A major aspect of simplicity is choosing long-term wellbeing over immediate gratification. Ralph Waldo

Emerson once said, *"Life is a journey, not a destination."* Therein lies the wisdom that rests at the very core of this debate between short-term and long-term contentment. Emerson was pointing out that we can find joy and fulfilment even when faced with obstacles and challenges if we view life as an ever-changing landscape, rather than simply the end result we desire. We all want happiness, but to achieve a lasting sense of peace and contentment, we must first recognise our broader purpose in life and then actively work toward it each day. Lasting contentment requires self-discipline so that our desires do not cause us anguish, stress, or regret over time due to poor choices.

While immediate gratification in some activities may provide temporary pleasure, only real commitment and patience are capable of bringing us true happiness and long-term contentment. Nowadays, people have become more aware of the need to practice self-discipline to achieve lasting contentment, and it's possible to set both meaningful short- and long-term goals. The short-term goals can help you stay focused, bringing a sense of satisfaction as you continue to take consistent steps toward your long-term vision.

An example of short-term goals might be improving your physical health through activities such as yoga or regular exercise. These can create a sense of joy and peace. Additionally, meditation and mindfulness techniques will help you stay calm and centred in difficult situations. Eating healthier foods and switching off from technology occasionally could also be short-term goals. In this way, self-discipline isn't just something that must be endured, it can be enjoyable when practiced in balance with other activities.

Service-oriented activities such as volunteering at a local charity or providing mentorship to high school students can also be short-term goals. These meaningful ways of helping others result in a sense of satisfaction that comes from knowing you are making an impact on another's life, while at the same time contributing positively to society.

To conclude, some short-term goals, such as going out drinking with friends or watching television, may provide immediate gratification but fail to provide long-term contentment. Other activities, such as community service, or improving your eating habits, are likely to lead you to a greater sense of contentment. In this way, a balance of well-chosen short-term goals can be enjoyable *and* contribute to achieving longer-term goals and lasting contentment.

Challenging Traditional Notions of Success

Despite popular belief, success does not necessarily require money or power. True progress comes from within by understanding your own strengths, weaknesses, and capabilities in terms of achieving self-actualisation, regardless of external norms or expectations set by society at large.

Success is traditionally viewed as a product of hard work, ambition, and financial gain. But, as Seneca believed, *"The time of life is too short for us to be able to enjoy anything from it truly worth having."* Rather than pursuing materialistic goals and outcomes, he advocated for leading lives driven by passion, purpose, and meaning.

For centuries, thinkers have challenged the traditional view of success by exploring the value of other qualities such as happiness and contentment in our lives. Aristotle believed, *"Happiness is the meaning and the purpose of life, the whole aim and end of human existence,"* while Zeno described his goal in life as being, *"Free from fear and guilt."*

Our society has started to reconsider how we define success. People are increasingly striving to lead meaningful lives through creative expression, personal relationships, and spiritual development, rather than status or money. As Marie Curie noted in reference to her own experience developing new scientific theories, *"Nothing in life is to be feared; it is only to be understood."* This shift toward understanding the value of true experiences over materialistic accomplishments has significantly improved quality of life for many because it means they can finally pursue their dreams and see them come alive without financial restraint or social pressure influencing their decisions.

Seneca emphasised that achieving lasting satisfaction requires an individual to align their values with their actions. When we look beyond economic earnings or career recognition as measures for success, we open ourselves to finding joy through our everyday actions instead of chasing temporary highs from external sources such as salary boosts or public praise. When we move away from traditional metrics of success toward something more holistic – such as living a fulfilling life – we make sure that every day counts toward something meaningful rather than toward an accumulation of wealth and status symbols.

Establishing productive habits and focusing on learning and growth allows an individual to thrive without resorting to measuring success by common metrics. Such a shift means that each day can contribute significantly toward fulfilling self-actualisation goals, instead of those that bring only short-term gratification.

Preserving Mental Sanity Through Simplicity

As life has its ups and downs, no matter our status or lifestyle choices, simplifying our lives can provide a respite from the chaos. It creates restorative spaces where we can relax and renew ourselves free from distractions detrimental to mental health, such as constant noise pollution or overstimulation from digital devices and social media platforms, etc. Albert Einstein once quipped, *"Everything should be as simple as possible, but no simpler."* In Max's case, making life simpler helped him find peace and contentment.

But what does this mean in practice? How do we go about simplifying our lives? The answer can be found in the philosophy of minimalism, meaning the pursuit of owning fewer possessions, living more intentionally with those possessions, and focusing on experiences instead of material items. By limiting ourselves to only those things that are essential – both physical objects and abstract concepts like thoughts and ideals – we may begin to reclaim a sense of clarity amidst complexity, or peace within a whirlwind world.

By focusing on simplicity rather than complexity, we can reclaim our mental sanity amidst life's chaotic fluxes. Leonidas Mavrides said, *"Simplicity is not the goal; it is the way."* This statement tells us that we need to actively seek out moments for contemplation and reflection among life's ever-changing tides of chaos if we are to find sanctuary. We cannot necessarily escape from life's complexities without first reclaiming a sense of calm within them – something that can only be achieved through finding simplicity where there is chaos.

When trying to solve a problem or explain something, choose the simplest solution available. Avoid overcomplicating matters and instead strive for simplicity to make solutions easier to understand. Einstein believed that this approach could be applied to all aspects of life from scientific theories to everyday occurrences, and that life can often be made simpler by breaking things down into their most basic forms. While the aim is to keep everything as straightforward and effortless as possible, enough complexity should be retained to ensure accuracy and correctness.

Simply put, this means that by focusing on simplicity rather than complexity, we can reclaim our mental sanity amidst life's chaotic fluxes, restoring a sense of peace within the hustle and bustle. To this end, actively seek out moments for contemplation and reflection.

Avoiding Overthinking

Overthinking is mentally exhausting and prevents you from finding peace within yourself as you ruminate on negative thoughts or worries about the future instead of living in and appreciating the present-day.

Overthinking can be a powerful force that holds you back in life and can even prevent you from reaching your fullest potential. Seneca wisely wrote: *"We suffer more often in imagination than in reality."* Overthinking can lead to worrying about things that may never happen or stressing about scenarios that will never come true, sapping your time and energy in the process.

To make the most of life, it's important to avoid overthinking. Excessive thinking can consume our minds and cause us to think negatively as we focus on everything that could go wrong instead of taking a step back and seeing the bigger picture. This can lead to making snap judgments and decisions based on fear rather than faith, and these can often work against us in the long run. As Mark Twain once wittily pointed out, *"I have been through some terrible things in my life, some of which actually happened."*

When faced with difficult situations, it is essential to take a step back and truly evaluate your options logically, instead of letting emotions or irrational thoughts take control. It was Nelson Mandela who said, *"It always seems impossible until it's done,"* emphasising the importance of taking measured actions toward goals and not allowing your fears to hinder progress. Instead of constantly overthinking what could go wrong, focus on what could go right.

Negative thinking can be a major obstacle in achieving success and reaching goals. To effectively avoid overthinking and negative thinking, it is important to employ strategies that help prevent your mind getting overwhelmed with unhelpful thoughts. Here are a few suggestions:

1. Practice mindfulness: Being mindful helps you to stay focused in the present moment and break away mentally from the cycle of worrying over what might happen in the future, or ruminating on things that have already happened. Taking a few moments to become aware of your thoughts and emotions can help you become more aware of your thought patterns, and to recognise when you are stuck in an unproductive spiral. You can then practice letting go of any negative thoughts.

2. Identify your triggers: Recognise which situations are likely to trigger negative thinking. This can help you anticipate them and prevent anxious thought patterns before they begin. Unhelpful triggers may include stressful situations or being around certain people who bring out your anxiety. Try to take control of these external influences by avoiding them whenever possible, or actively choosing positive people, activities, etc., instead.

3. Find healthy ways to let go of your worries: Trying to ignore negative thoughts doesn't always work, but finding healthy ways to let them go can be effective in releasing some of the stress that's causing

you to overthink in the first place. Writing down your worries, talking about them with someone supportive, going for a walk — try a few techniques and find whatever works best for you as a way of expressing your anxieties without letting them consume you. This will help relieve mental pressure from overthinking and give you more space for creative problem-solving.

By consistently practicing these strategies, you can focus on taking positive steps toward your goals and avoid getting caught up in harmful worry patterns that hold you back.

Mindfulness exercises are a great way to bring more awareness and intentionally be in the present moment, as opposed to getting lost in unhelpful thought patterns. Examples of mindfulness activities that you can practice include:

1. Meditation: Taking a few moments each day to sit quietly and focus on your breath or an affirmation can help boost feelings of calm and wellbeing while also helping you become aware of any thoughts that may be influencing your mindset in an unhelpful manner.
2. Mindful walking: Instead of mindlessly walking around, use this opportunity as a chance to tune into your body and environment by focusing on how your steps feel or noticing the scenery around you. This will help bring awareness to the present moment instead of just letting your mind wander off into unhelpful thinking patterns.

3. Body scan: In this exercise, you take time to focus on each part of your body and observe any sensations without judgment. This helps you pay attention to what is happening inside yourself instead of always being focused outwards. This in turn can be helpful for increasing self-awareness and letting go of unnecessary stress caused by overthinking.
4. Listening practice: Spend time listening deeply to even the smallest sound rather than playing background noises that you listen to passively. This encourages you to really take in what's going on around you, instead of being distracted from reality by all the mental chatter going through your head!

In summary, overthinking can have negative consequences, using time and energy and blocking you from achieving your goals. Strategies to avoid overthinking include mindfulness practices (meditation, walking, body scan, and listening exercises), identifying triggers to avoid, and learning techniques to let go of your worries.

Patience and Forgiveness

Living simply means evaluating priorities carefully so that greater attention is given to those matters which truly deserve it. This includes developing healthier relationships with others by cultivating tolerance, patience, and forgiveness. Learn to adopt these behaviours rather than make unfavourable assumptions that cause conflict. Such conflicts use precious energy and rarely have constructive outcomes.

Patience and forgiveness are vital qualities to cultivate. Doing so requires the need to foster an attitude of compassion for others. We must be willing to accept people's mistakes and be willing to forgive them. As Nelson Mandela once said, *"We must develop and maintain the capacity to forgive. He who is devoid of the power to forgive is devoid of the power to love."* This sentiment resonates strongly with Seneca's philosophy on cultivating patience in all aspects of life, and his belief that we must learn to give people grace even when it feels difficult or undeserved.

We can also draw strength from understanding that forgiveness does not mean condoning wrong behaviour, or excusing someone from responsibility for their words or actions. It means understanding and accepting someone without holding a grudge. Gandhi said, *"The weak can never forgive; forgiveness is an attribute of the strong."* To cultivate patience, we must identify our own faults, appreciate the differences among others, and make sure we don't lose sight of what really matters in the grand scheme of things.

By striving to develop this mindset, we become more capable of creating an environment where others feel safe enough to express themselves openly without fear of judgment or retaliation. This helps us foster stronger relationships with those around us by creating room for growth within each person, instead of perpetual conflict rooted in anger, frustration, or blame. True patience comes from taking a step back before responding rashly, recognising how small moments will add up over time into bigger issues if left unresolved, and working toward resolution rather than retribution, if possible.

Practicing patience without condoning wrong behaviour requires a balance between understanding and compassion on the one hand, and strong boundaries and clear communication on the other. It's important to recognise when someone has behaved inappropriately, but also to have empathy for why they behaved in such a way. Acknowledge their feelings or point of view before enforcing your boundaries or choosing to forgive them. This can help the individual learn to take responsibility for their actions instead of resorting to blaming or shaming.

Taking a step back and not reacting immediately when something has angered you is also practicing patience. Our emotions can be powerful drivers of our decisions, so it's important to practice deep breaths and mindfulness techniques to regulate them. Taking time before responding often allows us to approach any situation with more clarity, and provide meaningful solutions rather than rash reactions that can further fuel conflicts or misunderstanding.

Finally, staying firm in your values yet also open-minded enough to accept new perspectives will help facilitate productive conversations, as well as build stronger relationships based on trust and mutual respect. In Nelson Mandela's words, *"If you want peace you don't talk to your friends, you talk with your enemies."* Learning how to practice patience while still maintaining your values is essential in cultivating true connections with those around you.

When faced with difficult situations, it can be tempting to respond with anger or frustration, but these feelings are often misguided and only serve to further complicate things. By understanding that life is short, and that time is precious, we can recognise the value in taking the time ourselves to build relationships based on tolerance and mutual respect.

Forgiveness doesn't mean condoning wrong behaviour. Cultivating a mindset of grace, patience, and empathy instead of retribution helps create an atmosphere in which people feel safe to express themselves openly without fear. This gives us deeper insight into who they are, allowing us to form stronger bonds rooted in trust rather than constant tension due to anger and blame.

True Peace and Contentment

Peace and contentment are perhaps two of the most sought-after feelings in life, but they *can* be yours – as illustrated in Max's story. However, everyone's definition of peace and contentment is different, and it can be a long journey to discover your individual sense of these emotions. If a man is as poor as his ambitions, we must continue to strive for true peace and contentment, even if at times it seems out of reach.

The path to true inner peace begins with self-reflection. Achieving peace within yourself requires honesty. Be honest about your strengths and weaknesses so that the right changes can be made, and the right goals set to build satisfaction with your life over time. A great way to start this process is journaling as it helps formally document your thoughts, problems, challenges, victories, and other observations along the way. This can give you clarity on what you are working toward or transitioning away from in your life to move closer to attaining peace.

The second step is being mindful of how you spend your time. Max's refocus on more meaningful activities in life helped him to find true peace and contentment. Too often we get caught up in activities that don't serve us well in terms of bringing true happiness or satisfaction into our lives. Be aware that some things will be necessity-based (such as work) but too much focus on obligatory tasks can detract from more meaningful pursuits that may bring you a greater sense of joy and genuine relief from stress. Aristotle said, *"Pleasure in the job puts perfection in the work."* The meaning in these words is that you must also enjoy what you do, not just perform tasks because they need to be done. Engaging too much in leisure activities rather than developing yourself or becoming more knowledgeable is also unwise, indicating that it takes a balance of work and relaxation/leisure activities to lead you closer to finding inner peace.

Focusing on practical mindfulness is a very effective method of finding personal peace and contentment. Understanding how your mind perceives certain events will help determine which type of conscious models you use when approaching similar events again. This can help in dealing with difficult situations – such as conflicts – and avoiding escalation of confrontations.

The last step on this journey is to look inwardly to understand who you really are without external noise or influence, discover your passions, and prioritise them over societal norms or conventions. When you learn to open yourself fully, and to be free from negativity and irrationality, then true inner peace may have been achieved.

One of the best ways to tap into your passions and prioritise them over societal norms is to take some time for yourself away from the hustle and bustle of everyday life. Go somewhere quiet, such as a cabin in the woods, or a beachfront property, where you can have some much-needed peace and solitude. Spend time reflecting on what truly makes you happy, energised, and fulfilled, and ask yourself why those things give you joy or make you feel good. Once you have identified your passions or interests, begin researching ways to pursue them. You can explore different options for education, extracurricular activities, and hobbies that will help you develop those skills.

Another way to explore inner passions is to create an action plan that can be followed daily with small achievable goals. Creating a schedule for yourself with consistent time allocation for pursuing these passions will provide structure and motivation to continue seeking knowledge and understanding. Additionally, it is important to surround yourself with likeminded people who can offer advice and guidance along the journey toward finding your true purpose in life. Having relationships with individuals who share similar values provides another valuable resource that should be taken advantage of when possible. Lastly, don't forget to take breaks regularly – rest is just as important as action when it comes to following our dreams.

To find your own peace and contentment, you can use several strategies. Use self-reflection through journaling to document your thoughts, problems, and challenges, and identify your passions in life. Be aware of how you spend your time to maximise its meaningfulness and find a balance between work and other activities. Practice mindfulness, and understand who you are and your passions by taking time away from the bustle of life. When you've identified your passion, research how to pursue it and create an action plan to achieve this.

Lessons from Finding Peace and Contentment

Accept that life is limited in time and use it wisely. Live in the moment, have a deeper relationship with your inner self, and do something meaningful that will have a lasting impact beyond your own existence.

Release yourself from attachment to material possessions or wealth, and recognise the importance of relationships, meaningful conversations, moments of joy, and other intangible elements that make up your life.

Accept life's uncertainty and focus on what you can control: your attitude, behaviour, and actions. Focus on what can be gained from hardships, and practice self-compassion.

Live gratefully and accept where you are right now to find true peace and joy in your life, no matter how much or how little you possess.

Well-chosen short-term goals can be enjoyable and contribute to your longer-term goals and contentment.

Establishing productive habits and focusing on learning and growth allows an individual to thrive without resorting to measuring success from financial earnings or career recognition.

Focus on simplicity rather than complexity to restore a sense of peace within the hustle and bustle of life. Actively seek out moments for contemplation and reflection.

Overthinking can have negative consequences, using time and energy that will block you from achieving your goals. Strategies to avoid overthinking include mindfulness (meditation, walking, body scan, and listening exercises), identifying triggers to avoid, and learning techniques to let go of your worries.

Several strategies can help you find your own peace and contentment: self-reflection through journaling, identifying your passions in life, optimising the meaningful use of your time, and finding a balance between work and other activities. Practice mindfulness, and understand who you are and your passions by taking time away from the bustle of life. When you've identified your passion, research how to pursue it and create an action plan to achieve this.

Chapter 9

Appreciating Life's Unique Experiences

Once upon a time, there lived an old man called Henry who had experienced much in life. From his earliest days, he had sought out the unique and the extraordinary. He savoured each moment, aware that his time on Earth was limited.

As he grew older, he became increasingly aware of how fragile life was, and how no two moments would ever be exactly alike. He continued to embrace all that life could offer him while it lasted. He enjoyed exploring new places and revisiting old favourites, conversing with strangers, and meeting new friends, learning lessons from his mistakes, and using them as a foundation for growth. He valued every minute of his existence as though it were a precious gem meant to be polished and treasured for eternity. But, at the back of his mind, there was always a cloud looming, the knowledge that his time was finite and that he wouldn't always exist to enjoy these moments.

Then one day, something happened that changed his perspective on life. While out walking on a warm summer morning, Henry passed by some local children playing in their front yard. They were laughing and shouting with joy. They weren't worrying about a future that might not exist. As he continued on his way, he reflected on the beauty of their innocence, and marvelled at how oblivious these small souls were to the fragility of their lives.

It was then that he realised something: despite its complexity and vastness, life is quite simple. Each experience lends itself to another unique adventure that can never be repeated or replaced. Appreciating life's unique experiences before they slip away is so important. Life is truly too special not to be cherished while on Earth!

With this newfound wisdom in tow, Henry returned home determined to continue living life with every breath, even if only for a few more years, months, or days, appreciating its unique experiences before they slipped away forever.

Embracing the Fragility of Life

We often spend our days chasing after an ideal life that will never truly arrive, unable to accept the uncertainty and fragility of life. However, by appreciating how temporary and fleeting all experiences are, we can discover a newfound depth and appreciation for everything we encounter in life.

We can often forget in our busy lives just how fragile life is. Seneca said, *"Life is not long, and too much of it must not be spent in idle deliberation."* By accepting the delicate nature of life, we can live each moment more fully and appreciate its true value. In the words of John Muir, *"In every walk with nature one receives far more than he seeks."* This serves as a reminder that life will always reward you with something new and wonderful if you simply allow yourself to become present within its grace and open your eyes.

What follows from this understanding is an appreciation of every moment as unique and fleeting, both hardships and joys alike. When we pause to recognise the impermanence of all things, we awaken to a new level of presence and understanding in our lives. We can learn to accept difficulty, not as an obstacle to overcome, but as part of a greater journey – one that passes away swiftly like a dream in the night sky.

Ultimately, by coming to terms with the fact that our days may be few, we can finally take pleasure in living each day more deeply than ever before – learning from moments both good and bad and cherishing each precious breath as if it may be our last.

Instead of fighting against fate or struggling against absence, it is essential for us to understand that everything is bound to change eventually. There is no point getting attached to something certain to leave. However, this understanding can also help us create powerful memories that bring joy right until the end without holding back if we live in the present moment.

The concept of impermanence, or the understanding that all things are changing and will eventually succumb to time, is a central tenet of Stoic philosophy. This idea is deeply connected with an acceptance of the nature of life and its transience. To surrender to this truth can be difficult at times, as significant effort must be made to move away from what was once familiar and safe. However, by embracing the flux of existence, you open yourself up to freedom and possibility.

As stressed by author Pema Chödrön, *"In any moment the universe is perfectly balanced; everything changes and is in flux. This stability in instability doesn't mean we are lost or without direction; it simply means things don't remain static – they evolve and adapt according to conditions."* Understanding this allows for conscious navigation through life's ever-changing landscape, enabling individuals to embrace growth in spite of surrounding uncertainty.

Seneca also noted that *"...all our wisdom is contained in recognising how fleeting and trivial are all things which fascinate nonsensical minds,"* suggesting a need for perspective when faced with change. Rather than allowing these external forces to take control of our lives, it is important to remember that while some elements may be beyond our power – such as aging and death – there remains enough free will under our governance to choose our actions and reactions toward each situation we face.

Accepting impermanence involves coming into harmony with change; finding peace amidst fluctuating times by recognising both their potential for growth as well as the ultimate disposition toward decay that all things share. As philosopher Alan Watts pointed out, *"Impermanence means you can no longer rely on safety – you have no choice but to go into life fully aware."* If you do, you can learn to let go gracefully while being ever mindful of making each moment count.

Alan Watts was an influential British philosopher who advocated for living life with a sense of adventure and courage. He believed that our lives are best lived when we let go of the illusion of permanence and instead embrace the dynamism of impermanence. Watts insightfully reframed impermanence as something that is empowering, rather than limiting or intimidating. His philosophy encourages us to be present in each moment without expecting it to last forever; to find joy in uncertainty and motion. We need to accept that creative potential lies within the ebbs and flows of life, and impermanence can provide us with a sense of freedom from the constraints of expectations and obligations placed upon us by ourselves or others. It is through this understanding that we can then truly appreciate each passing moment for what it is, allowing moments – however beautiful or painful – to pass without feeling overwhelmed by them.

Impermanence can be challenging to understand, but there are tangible practices you can adopt to better accept that nothing lasts forever. Here are some of the ways you can cultivate acceptance of impermanence:

1. Take control of your time: Be mindful of how you choose to spend your moments. Make conscious decisions about what really matters to you and try to invest more of your time into those activities or relationships.
2. Celebrate the moment: Appreciate each moment for what it is without expecting it to last forever. Find joy in the uncertainty, and beauty in the fleeting nature of life's experiences.
3. Connect with others: Reach out to close friends and family members when times get tough and

remember that although nothing lasts forever, we still have one another as constants in our lives.

4. Practice gratitude: Gratitude helps us gain perspective on where we have been and what we have currently, enabling us to move through life's changes with far more ease than if we were constantly focusing on what we lack or don't yet have.

Accepting impermanence is an ongoing process, one that requires patience and compassion toward ourselves as we learn to appreciate change rather than dread it. Managing your time wisely for meaningful activities, celebrating moments, connecting with others, and practicing gratitude will all help you to accept the impermanence of life.

Accepting Change

The beauty in life lies in its inconsistency. If everything stayed still and unchanging, our lives would be mundane and lacking in significance. But when things don't go as planned and chaos ensues, it is up to us to embrace the turbulence and find meaning in what we learn along the way.

Change and turbulence have long been seen as great sources of strength and growth by influential thinkers such as Seneca who believed, *"Whatever the mind seeks to acquire or keep, it obtains only by struggle."* But in a world of relentless change, it can be difficult to maintain perspective and find meaning amid such upheaval. To do so requires taking a step back and remembering the reasons behind your courage – remembering that life is short. While it is easy to get discouraged in times of turbulence and chaos, it is important to remember that these situations serve a greater purpose: they challenge us, test our resilience, and help us become better versions of ourselves.

To understand this concept better, we need to consider other thoughts leaders' perspectives on the topic. Steve Jobs once said, *"You can't connect the dots looking forward; you can only connect them looking backward."* What he meant by this is that without looking into the past for context and clarity, we cannot truly progress in our current circumstances. To make sense of your present situation, you must revisit your history and reflect on your experiences.

In fact, Friedrich Nietzsche, strongly believed, *"He who has a why to live for can bear almost any how,"* suggesting that it takes a clear understanding of your goals to maintain focus and make sense out of turbulent times. Understanding the *why* behind tough decisions can give us more insight into how they fit in with our lives and purposes. For example, the *why* behind a difficult decision to leave a job may have been wanting to pursue better career opportunities or gain new skills. Understanding the why for such decisions can help you avoid regrets and embrace your new path. Similarly, when faced with major changes in life that require letting go of old habits or routines, understanding the reason for the change makes it easier to accept and move on.

Navigating life's ever-changing landscape can be a tricky endeavour as it involves learning to move with the flow of change rather than against it. Here are some strategies for doing just that:

1. Embrace uncertainty: The key to embracing life's ever-changing landscape is accepting uncertainty. Rather than resisting change, accept that an element of unpredictability exists and learn to adapt accordingly.

2. Cultivate mindfulness: Mindfulness helps us stay present in each moment without getting lost in worrying about the future or ruminating on the past. It enables us to better respond to life's changes with clarity and grace.

3. Practice reflection: Reflect on the change and how it fits into your goals and values.

4. Seek opportunities for growth: Change can often bring new and exciting opportunities for growth and development if we're willing to look for them. See every shift as a chance to develop yourself further, no matter how small it may seem at first glance.

5. Let go of expectations: Though difficult, letting go of expectations can be beneficial in allowing yourself more space to explore different possibilities, or take on unexpected challenges without feeling guilty or overwhelmed when things don't go according to plan.

6. Focus on what you can control. For example, set boundaries and create new routines that will help you adjust more easily.

7. Find positive ways of coping: For example, talk things over with friends or engage in activities that make you happy.

8. Maintain balance: Take time for both you and your relationships. Practicing self-care, prioritising

quality time with loved ones, and learning to take a step back when needed can all help with developing a sense of stability in an otherwise unpredictable situation.

9. Focus on the positive: Navigating life's changing landscape can be stressful and often difficult, but it also presents us with opportunities to learn and grow that we wouldn't have without it. Try to look on the bright side whenever possible, focusing on what you have gained or can gain from the given situation rather than what you may have lost in the process.

10. Celebrate accomplishments: Don't forget to congratulate yourself on small victories and recognise how far you've come since the day the changes first began. Celebrating your successes, no matter how large or small they may be, will give you greater motivation to keep going and work toward adapting to whatever comes next.

Change is inevitable in life and it can be difficult, but it serves as a challenge to develop your resilience. There are many strategies you can use to help you through, such as meditation, reflection, letting go of expectations, focusing on what you can control, and positive thinking.

Challenging Your Comfort Zone

Fear tends to paralyse us, hindering our ability to reach our full potential. But what if instead of staying in a safe comfort zone, we were willing to challenge ourselves and embrace new experiences? Turning discomfort into an opportunity is effectively a process of reframing and reinterpreting, allowing us to break out of our comfort zone and become stronger individuals.

In the words of Seneca, *"We suffer more often in imagination than in reality."* The message here is that we tend to shy away from unfamiliar things, often out of fear or apprehension. But what if we could learn to use unfamiliarity to our advantage instead of avoiding it? The truth is that discomfort can often lead us to think outside the box, revealing opportunities that we wouldn't have found otherwise.

The key is found in learning how to separate our fears from reality and focus on the potential opportunities that exist in uncomfortable situations. Aristotle said, *"It is during our darkest moments that we must focus to see the light."* By forcing ourselves out of our own comfort zones and embracing new experiences, we open ourselves up to different ways of thinking and problem-solving. If you challenge yourself on a daily basis by doing something uncomfortable, eventually you get used to feeling comfortable with being uncomfortable.

Difficulty and challenge can act as steppingstones for growth and personal development. Furthermore, accepting challenges can create unique life experiences that would not have been available otherwise. As writer Robert Louis Stephenson explained, *"To have faith is to be strong – strong enough to trust unthinkingly in the power which churns up our lives with strange surprises."*

This idea can also be applied in business settings, where unfamiliarity can promote positive change and growth.

Entrepreneur Seth Godin voiced this concept when he said, *"The opposite of comfort isn't trouble. It's possibility. To get from here to there requires abandoning complacency and taking risks instead of avoiding risk or waiting until you're certain you won't fail."* By choosing to see obstacles as opportunities rather than roadblocks, we open ourselves up to different ways of thinking that can lead to success.

Taking risks and embracing unfamiliarity are not easy tasks, but they offer tremendous rewards if done correctly. Businesswoman Mary Kay Ash summed this concept up perfectly in saying, *"We must have courage... We must make the best use of time at our disposal... The difference between successful people and others is their perception about uncomfortable situations... They know that without discomfort nothing comes into being."* Difficulties will come no matter what, but by learning to view them as opportunities, we can take control over our path to personal growth.

As we all know too well, life itself is full of trials and tribulations that can leave us feeling scared and overwhelmed. But if we take some time to reframe these experiences as opportunities for growth, then they become areas where we can find strength and personal development. As businessman Jim Rohn stated, *"The key is not only to be willing to accept discomfort as normal but also welcome it as an opportunity for growth."*

While it might feel easier in the short term to avoid confronting discomfort head on, true fulfilment comes from facing those uncomfortable moments with courage, and transforming them into steppingstones of progress. This is a process that requires putting aside fear and taking charge by actively seeking out unfamiliar situations so that we can grow in knowledge and experience. In the words of bestselling author Paulo Coelho, *"Everyone should try once in life this type of experience – turning what appears dangerous into something beneficial."*

So, don't be afraid to step outside your comfort zone. Embrace unfamiliar experiences to reach new heights of success. By choosing to view discomfort as an opportunity for growth, you can create unique life experiences that will stay with you forever.

Passionate Living

A healthy acceptance of impermanence should not stifle creativity or lead us down a path of apathy. Instead, this understanding should be used to invigorate our passions and drive us forward on our journey toward meaningful living every day. Etty Hillesum voiced this beautifully when she said, *"A new life awaits you, an unknown world full of possibilities... Dare take your chance!"*

The importance of passion cannot be overstated. It provides purpose and rationale when our circumstances feel uncertain. The trick lies in learning how to harness passion even amidst inevitable change and impermanence, thereby allowing access to fulfilling experiences even during difficult times. In Helen Keller's words, *"Life is either a daring adventure or nothing at all."*

Learning to appreciate the beauty and richness of life itself and how precious moments can be maximised into something meaningful or satisfying is of key importance. Albert Einstein once said, *"The most beautiful thing we can experience is the mysterious. It is the source of all true art and science."* Moreover, what resonates with humans on an emotional level often gives us something substantial beyond our own desires — something worth pursuing.

Seneca's writings also remind us that life should be measured by how much joy we derive from each moment. As the ancient Greek proverb advises, "Know thyself." Once you know yourself deeply through reflection and taking calculated risks, you'll realise that passionate living was always within your reach. This requires self-awareness, asking yourself where your passions lie, and what will bring you great satisfaction in every area of living: relationships, work/study endeavours, and activities that help maintain physical health and mental clarity.

At its core, life should be treated with respect but also with an openness for exploration and change. Passion comes from taking risks — trying new experiences even when failure seems possible. Fearful resignation must be avoided as there's so much available to you if you have the courage to pursue it. Here are examples of five risks worth taking to live passionately.

1. Trying something completely new and out of your comfort zone: Take a dance class, learn a new language, or take up a hobby that you have never done before.

2. Pursuing a passion or career path despite the risk of failure: Find something that excites you and pour yourself into it, regardless of what others think.
3. Living in another country for a while: Live in a location that challenges your perceptions, helps you grow, and opens up opportunities that couldn't have been found at home.
4. Taking on creative projects with no guarantee of success: Express yourself through art, writing, filmmaking, or any other form of creative media, and put yourself out there without knowing whether it will succeed or fail.
5. Opening yourself up to relationships with people who are different to you: Get to know people from different cultures, backgrounds, and experiences. These connections can help bring out the best in everyone involved!

You can also look to nature for inspiration on how best to embrace passionate living. Nature has both violent storms and peaceful sunsets. You must learn to find happiness in both small moments and larger victories alike, always recognising what brings you joy, while also preparing yourself for what lies ahead beyond your control.

Finding joy in small moments can mean taking a few minutes to appreciate a simple pleasure such as the beauty of nature, spending time with loved ones, or savouring the taste and flavour of a favourite food. It could also mean having an appreciation for small successes in life such as completing a task that you have been working on for some time or gaining clarity on a difficult problem you have been struggling with.

Larger victories are those goals we set for ourselves that may require more effort and dedication to realise, but are immensely rewarding when achieved. Examples of larger victories include getting a promotion at work, completing university studies, learning a new language or skill, achieving financial independence, travelling to new countries and cultures, starting your own business, and launching new projects you believe in passionately.

So, to achieve passionate living, accept your impermanence and appreciate the beauty and richness of life; find contentment from within through reflection and self-awareness; take risks to try new things; appreciate nature, and moments and victories large and small.

Reconnecting with Nature and Simplicity

Too often we overlook nature's healing power when trying to make sense of daily anxieties. Reconnecting with nature allows us to break away from the chaos of everyday life and appreciate the wonders within it that have existed since time immemorial.

Taking a step outside and being present in nature has been scientifically proven to reduce stress levels due to the calming effects its physical presence has on our minds and bodies. Studies show that even just small acts such as taking a few deep breaths in a park or feeling dew beneath your feet whilst walking through an open field can significantly improve overall wellbeing, allowing you to relax more easily and refocus on what matters most.

Humans have always been connected to nature. From the dawn of civilisation, our ancestors hunkered down amongst trees and seas as they established their dwellings. They felt both comfort and awe in the presence of the natural world and that same emotion is still felt today. Seneca said, *"Nature never ceases to amaze; its beauty is timeless and eternal."* He knew that the bond between humans and nature was an important one, and one we must never forget to nurture. Henry David Thoreau echoed this sentiment when he said, *"I went to the woods because I wished to live deliberately, to front only the essential facts of life, and see if I could learn what it had to teach, and not when I came to die discover that I had not lived."*

Whether you believe in connecting with something greater than mankind or simply love being outdoors, spending time outside will bring you closer to nature. Reconnecting with nature is about more than just mental health, it's about recognising our interconnection within this vast universe, and feeling at home amidst all its beauty.

Epicurus said, *"We are born once and cannot be born twice, but as long as we live, we can recreate ourselves."* Nowhere does this notion ring truer than in our relationship with nature. Reconnecting with the natural environment offers us an opportunity to appreciate the world around us and provides comfort in its simplicity, a reminder of life's beauty regardless of our day-to-day struggles.

Our ancestors sought solace in nature for centuries. From ancient poets such as Homer, who spoke of the power of seaside strolls for relaxation purposes, to medieval writers such as Dante Alighieri, who used nature as metaphors for his spiritual writings, many have found escapism within its beauty. In more modern times, well-known figures such as Mahatma Gandhi and Alice Walker have shared their belief in the comforts of being in nature. Gandhi spoke of finding solace in nature's beauty when nothing else could soothe, and Walker of finding solace in nature that cannot be found elsewhere. These thoughts highlight the importance of immersing ourselves in raw beauty when looking to remove anxiety from our lives.

In today's busy world, it can be easy to get lost in the hustle and bustle, forgetting to truly connect with our environment. We're surrounded by technology that does so much for us but keeps us removed from that which sustains us naturally, our environment. In our technology-driven world, it can seem impossible to establish a healthy balance between modern life and nature. However, it is possible with a few simple strategies that can help you to reconnect with the natural environment, even in the hectic world of today.

First and foremost, making time for nature during your leisure activities can bring more balance into your life. Taking walks in the park, bird watching, or exploring local forests will deepen your connection with nature and provide you with much needed respite from city life. Additionally, investing in outdoor activities such as camping or gardening will help ground you, encouraging stillness, and create harmony between technology and nature. Taking regular walks in the park or hiking up a mountain can help us renew this connection, allowing us to take comfort in simplicity while finding peace among grandeur.

Taking note of natural surroundings when commuting can also foster appreciation for nature while going about daily tasks. Taking a moment to focus on nearby trees or plants while getting from point A to point B may not seem significant, but this small act can cultivate a greater connection between everyday life and the powerful force of nature.

Further, making small changes in the way you use technology may help find this balance. Limiting the amount of time spent on social media or using software applications specifically designed to reduce smartphone usage are two steps to reduce time spent on screen, while still allowing you to stay connected with friends and colleagues. If these steps feel too challenging, setting boundaries such as not using phones after 7pm or leaving phones at home when running errands will help keep both work commitments and life obligations balanced with quality time spent enjoying nature's beauty.

From calming effects on mental health to providing guidance during spiritual journeys, reconnecting with nature is a powerful tool for finding peace amongst daily anxieties. Whether you take time out alone or bring loved ones along for the experience, embracing moments spent outside will increase your appreciation for each day. Taking part in activities such as bird watching or simply taking a walk in nature allows you to remember your place within its vastness, and find peace amidst chaos.

Establishing Momentum on Life's Journey

Impermanence should remind us that even though each moment must come to pass eventually, they possess tremendous potential when connected together over time into a long-term journey full of purpose and moments achieved together with loved ones.

The lesson of life is that we ought to be making the most of it, no matter how short it feels. The key then lies in creating moments that enable sustainable progress throughout our journey. This can be achieved by getting into the habit of taking meaningful steps forward each day to form lasting habits that will serve as pillars for our growth in the future. When written down and visualised regularly, these small goals become larger than they appear initially, and provide a roadmap for success.

Statistician Nassim Taleb described this concept in saying, *"Progression means you advance every day even if by a fractional amount."* Seemingly insignificant daily actions can have profound results over time when plotted out sequentially. This becomes especially evident when combined with other personal efforts such as education or self-improvement practices like journaling or meditation.

A successful strategy for establishing momentum necessitates purposeful action combined with an unwavering commitment from within yourself. The motivation must come from within rather than from external sources. We all know what happens when life throws curveballs, so it is essential that our resolve is concrete enough to withstand any obstacles placed before us during our journey through life. Always understand *why* you are doing what you are doing, so that you maintain your course whatever comes your way.

Creating a daily routine is an effective way to help work toward achieving your goals. A routine helps keep you focused and on track. Start by setting measurable goals and then create a plan of action that fits within your current lifestyle. This could include tasks such as reading, writing, or planning out each day before starting it. Scheduling specific blocks of time to focus on certain activities can also help increase productivity and focus.

In addition to goal-oriented activities, incorporate some self-care into your routine. Taking breaks throughout the day to relax, meditate, or spend time with loved ones will help reduce stress and refocus your mind when you return to working on your goals.

No matter how large or small the task at hand may be, a consistent routine will help ensure progress is made toward accomplishing whatever goals have been set. The journey may seem long at times, but remember that commitment today leads to growth tomorrow. Establishing momentum takes time but can lead to lasting success if done with patience and determination!

Reward systems can also be useful when trying to establish momentum on a journey. A simple way of doing this is setting milestones along the way and working toward them. When they are achieved, there is something tangible to celebrate. It's important to recognise progress, even if it is incremental. Treat yourself for completing small tasks as well as reaching bigger goals. For example, take time off after achieving a major milestone.

In reminding yourself why you are doing what you are doing, you also provide motivation in times of doubt. Write down your ultimate goal and find ways to stay fired up about it to help keep you on track and drive results, no matter what the circumstances.

Identifying external sources of motivation can be an effective way to stay focused and committed to your goals. This could include connecting with likeminded individuals or attending workshops or seminars that promote personal growth. Participating in a mastermind group or having a mentor may also help hold you accountable and provide a different perspective on how to approach certain tasks.

Lastly, it can be helpful to set up an arrangement with someone to check in and provide progress updates every week. Having someone hold you accountable for persevering makes staying motivated much easier. Having an outside perspective can also prove beneficial in terms of helping you find solutions when needed. Establishing a clear line of communication not only helps ensure progress is made, but also provides a positive reinforcement system that encourages growth over time!

Achieving your meaningful goals in life requires momentum on a long journey. Each step or small task contributes toward the larger goals. However, you need a roadmap to help you persevere, and commitment and motivation from within. Plan a daily, consistent routine, with measurable goals, milestones, and rewards, and include breaks to meditate, spend time with loved ones, and relax. Use external support to bolster your motivation; for example, have a mentor monitor your progress and provide an objective perspective, or attend workshops for personal growth.

Quality Over Quantity

As difficult as it may seem at first, try to narrow focus onto those actions and daily regimes which have most meaning, then concentrate diligently on pursuing them to excellence to derive the greatest value.

When pursuing goals, most people focus on quantity. They strive for larger numbers and bigger accomplishments. As a result, they often sacrifice their own wellbeing, and in turn produce unsatisfactory outcomes. It is more valuable to pause and assess our goals from a perspective of quality rather than quantity. Are the things we are striving for worth our efforts? Will the results make us happy?

Albert Einstein echoed a similar sentiment when he said, *"Try not to become a man of success, but rather try to become a man of value."* Those who prioritise meaningful endeavours over superficial achievements will come out ahead in the long run. Pursuing projects that are aligned with your values aligns them with true riches – that which brings fulfilment and satisfaction – not necessarily fame or money.

Stephen Covey stated this point quite effectively when he said, *"We need to think 'quality' rather than 'quantity'.*

The key is not how much you do, but how much love you put into what you do." Quality takes effort and attention to detail; it requires self-awareness so you can tune into what matters most in any endeavour. Pay close attention to your actions. Doing so will result in less time wasted on trying things out with little end result or joy.

Choosing quality over quantity should be applied not only in activities related to work or career advancement, but also when deciding which hobbies and projects to pursue. Spend your days focusing on important tasks while avoiding superfluous ones. This will prevent you from becoming overwhelmed by too many commitments or activities simply because they appear potentially useful or fun at first glance.

In conclusion, choosing quality over quantity will help you to lead a more fulfilled life by ensuring that you pursue only those goals that bring real meaning into your life, instead of attempting too many ventures simultaneously with little regard for their intrinsic value or ability to bring lasting satisfaction.

Here are some strategies you can use to prioritise quality over quantity:

1. Prioritise what matters most. Take an inventory of your current commitments and prioritise those activities that bring you the most meaning or joy. These should be given more attention than others.
2. Step back and reflect. Before jumping into a task, take a step back and analyse whether the task is aligned with your values and brings true happiness or satisfaction.

3. Get rid of distractions. Distractions (or activities with less meaning to you) can make it harder to stay focused on important tasks, so work diligently to identify and eliminate those that are preventing you from achieving your desired outcomes quickly yet effectively while avoiding burnout in the process.

Avoid trying to do everything, and then doing everything poorly by taking too much on. Instead, focus on quality over quantity. This involves reflecting deeply on what the most meaningful priorities in life are for you, and removing the distractions or less meaningful activities.

Cherishing Every Memory

The ability to reflect fondly on the past without regretting mistakes is crucial to developing a mature outlook. In his essays, Seneca discussed how life passes us by at such a rate that we often fail to truly appreciate and savour each moment. Each moment should be cherished, and life should not be taken for granted.

At each turn in life, it is important to pause and reflect on where we have been and where we are going. Too often we become so engrossed in what lies ahead that we forget to look back at all the moments that have brought us this far. A reflection on times past can provide insight into future choices as well as help bring perspective on current decisions. As poet William Wordsworth wrote: *"Though nothing can bring back the hour of splendour in the grass, of glory in the flower; we will grieve not, rather find strength in what remains behind."*

Cherishing every memory and reflection along the way can lead to happiness. We need to take time away from our daily hustle to appreciate both ourselves and those around us, so that when faced with life's end, we don't regret past moments left unenjoyed or unappreciated.

We can only be present for what is happening right now. However, our thoughts often wander away from each moment as we dream and plan for our future. This isn't necessarily a bad thing, in fact, having goals and working to achieve them can bring tremendous joy and satisfaction, but if we are not mindful of how we are spending our present moments, we may be disappointed later.

Ralph Waldo Emerson said, *"Life is like a train journey – one arrives at some stations earlier than others – but every station gives us an opportunity to reflect on where we've been and where we're going."* From this perspective, life becomes more about savouring all the stops along the way instead of constantly pushing forward in search of a destination that may not exist.

Cherishing every memory and reflection along the way should also be accompanied by understanding that mistakes are part of life's mosaic, just as much as successes are. Accepting responsibility for our mistakes without judgment or guilt can help foster self-acceptance while also leading toward personal growth and maturity. As psychiatrist Carl Jung said, *"Every experience has its own value – whatever happens has its richness; even failure is nothing more than a new starting point."*

Each moment can become an opportunity to appreciate where we have come from with gratitude, while recognising what lies ahead. In this way, living with awareness every day will help us create fuller lives despite knowing full well the shortness of life. Achieving a fuller life despite its shortness may seem daunting, but it is possible if we take the time to savour each moment and appreciate every reflection along the way. We must look back at how far we have come and use our past experiences – both successes and mistakes – as lessons to strengthen our character and propel us forward.

By taking a few moments to stop, reflect, and enjoy all that has been given to us, we can create a lasting connection with ourselves, our loved ones, and the world around us. We must remember that no matter what happens in life, each experience has value. Henry learned the value of cherishing his memories of moments when he reflected on the children enjoying their moments, oblivious to the shortness of life.

It is also important to live with intention so that when life's journey ends, we can look back with a sense of accomplishment and satisfaction. If we are intentional about how we spend our time here on Earth and strive toward meaningful goals based on our unique values, rather than external expectations or pressures, then we can find joy in our pursuits even though life may end too soon.

Enjoy each moment, and reflect on and cherish all the moments that have brought you to where you are, even the failures that bring learning for the future.

Going forwards, live with intention, working toward your meaningful goals.

Cultivating Gratitude for Life's Ephemeral Moments

Life is fleeting, making it important to recognise the beauty of ephemeral moments and cultivate a sense of gratitude for them. Ephemeral moments need not only be enjoyed alone, but can also be appreciated by sharing with others.

Although an experience may seem insignificant at the time, it's worth will increase over time. In other words, our appreciation of moments grows richer as we look back. Philosopher Jean-Paul Sartre wrote: *"Everything has been figured out except how to live."* With these words, he reminds us that no matter how hard we try, life could end at any moment without warning, so we should take every opportunity to find joy in small things.

Gratitude for life's ephemeral moments allows us the freedom to carry on living with joy despite the uncertainty of life's end. By recognising and appreciating the beauty in transient experiences – such as a sunrise or a conversation – we emphasise their importance and create meaning in an uncertain world. One way to do this is through mindfulness exercises such as meditation that help you focus on what truly matters in life, even if those things are fleeting, instead of getting lost in the distractions of day-to-day concerns.

Cultivating gratitude requires us to step back and appreciate what makes life special, rather than allowing future worries to take away our present enjoyment. Zen philosopher Thich Nhat Hanh once said, *"Feelings come and go like clouds easily seen but difficult to hold onto,"* reminding us that only by truly paying attention can we catch hold of these feelings before they pass by forever.

Though moments come and go too quickly to ever catalogue or count, they can still bring us great joy if we take the time to immerse ourselves in them. Writer Maya Angelou wrote: *"Be present in all things and thankful for all things."* Gratitude is an emotion that can be harnessed to help us learn how to make the most of every fleeting moment.

19th-century philosopher Arthur Schopenhauer proposed that contemplation is key to living a contented life in saying, *"We should now and then review our past life by thinking over every part, consider what has been well and what ill."* To contemplate our experiences with appreciation rather than regret anchors us in reality. We should have no regrets for lost opportunities, and no feelings of dissatisfaction with what we have achieved.

The notion that our lives are finite allows us not only to feel grateful for each passing moment, but also gives us permission to choose which moments deserve our attention. Through this process of 'selective savouring,' we can tap into great sources of joy even in times of hardship. Cultivating gratitude for life's ephemeral moments gives us solace on an individual level and peace on an interpersonal level.

Selective savouring is an approach to appreciating life's moments, large and small. It involves consciously engaging with experiences that bring joy, contentment, and satisfaction, while disregarding or letting go of those that cause distress or discomfort. This strategy seeks to promote a greater awareness of the present moment, and brings a sense of appreciation in place of regret.

When we practice selective savouring, we acknowledge the power of each passing moment – no matter how brief – and take hold of it with gratitude instead of dwelling on what could have been. The idea is to focus on the things that bring us joy without getting distracted by external events or circumstances that might cloud our perception of reality.

This process can be broken down into three steps: actively noticing what brings pleasure, investing time in these moments, and then reflecting on them afterwards. Taking the time to engage in this kind of thoughtful appreciation encourages us to make use of every moment we are given, and helps us cultivate an attitude of thankfulness for life's gifts.

Cherishing life's fleeting moments is a great way to make the most of our time here on Earth. Here are some tips to help you get started:

• Be present: Be present in each moment, no matter how small. Focus all your attention on what you're doing; actively engaging with the task can bring great joy and appreciation.

- Slow down: Find ways to slow down throughout the day and take time to enjoy the little things. Taking walks, reading books, or simply enjoying a cup of tea can be excellent opportunities to appreciate life's moments.
- Take up a hobby: Pursuing activities that align with your interests and passions can offer much needed relief from everyday stressors, and help you stay connected to your values and purpose in life.
- Take note of what brings fulfilment: Keeping track of activities that bring you pleasure helps you identify these precious moments more quickly. Writing these experiences down or sharing them with friends can act as an effective reminder to always strive for joy in each passing moment.

Life is fleeting, making it important to recognise the beauty of ephemeral moments and cultivate a sense of gratitude for them. Be present in the moment, slow down in your daily life, pursue activities that align with your values and passions, and keep track of activities that bring you happiness so that you know how to strive for meaning in life.

Lessons from Appreciating Life's Unique Experiences

Take pleasure in living each day deeply – learning from moments both good and bad, and cherishing each precious breath as if it may be your last.

Learn to accept impermanence by managing your time wisely for meaningful activities, celebrating moments, connecting with others, and practicing gratitude.

Change is inevitable in life and serves as a challenge to develop your resilience, which can sometimes be difficult. Reflect on the causes of, or reasons for, change to understand their meaning, and use strategies such as meditation, reflection, letting go of expectations, focusing on what you can control, and positive thinking to help you accept change.

Don't be afraid to step outside your comfort zone; embrace unfamiliar experiences to reach new heights of success. By choosing to view discomfort as an opportunity for growth, you can create unique life experiences that will stay with you forever.

Accept your impermanence and appreciate the beauty and richness of life to live with passion; find contentment from within through reflection and self-awareness; take risks to try new things; appreciate nature, and every moment and victory, big and small.

Reconnect with nature to escape daily anxieties. Walk in the woods or simply notice nature around you to help appreciate your place in the universe and find peace amidst chaos.

To keep momentum on your journey to a meaningful life, acknowledge that each step or small task contributes toward the larger goals. Plan a daily, consistent routine, with measurable goals, milestones, and rewards, and include breaks to meditate, spend time with loved ones, and relax. Use external support to bolster your motivation. For example, have a mentor monitor your progress and provide an objective perspective, or attend workshops for personal growth.

Avoid trying to do everything, and then end up doing everything poorly by taking too much on. Instead, focus on quality over quantity. This involves reflecting deeply on what the most meaningful priorities in life are for you and removing the distractions or less meaningful activities.

Enjoy each moment and reflect on and cherish all the moments that have brought you to where you are, even the failures that bring with them learning for the future. Going forwards, live with intention, working toward your meaningful goals.

Life is fleeting, making it important to recognise the beauty of ephemeral moments and cultivate a sense of gratitude for them. Be present in the moment, slow down in your daily life, pursue activities that align with your values and passions, and keep track of activities that bring you happiness so that you know how to strive for meaning in life.

Chapter 10

In Conclusion

Charles had a passion for living life to its fullest. He knew that the real key to making his life meaningful was to take risks and try new things, rather than sitting back and waiting for opportunities to land in his lap.

He started off by taking up hobbies he never thought he would enjoy, such as hiking and painting. Although daunting at first, Charles soon found joy in even the smallest of things. This newfound appreciation for the world around him eventually became an integral part of his life.

In his later years, Charles looked back on his life with pride and joy. He had taken risks throughout his entire life that led him to have experiences filled with adventure and discovery. Though there were times when things didn't go as planned, Charles viewed each challenge as an opportunity to learn something new about himself and the world around him.

He understood that living a meaningful life meant taking chances and pushing himself beyond what was comfortable or familiar. Instead of using fear as a crutch, Charles shifted focus onto positive thoughts of possibility and potential growth. By doing this, he learned powerful lessons about how to truly embrace life's ups and downs with courage and optimism.

Charles's journey taught him one important truth: when you strive for something greater than yourself, it creates meaning through moments of personal growth – no matter how small they may seem at first glance. He cherished every single moment spent pursuing his passions, knowing that each step forward was what made it worth it in the end.

Living a Meaningful Life

Living a meaningful life refers to finding purpose and passion throughout life. It involves reflecting deeply on the values that matter most and striving to live those values in all areas of life. This can include exploring the concept of what it means to be alive, the importance of relationships, spirituality and religion, understanding your own mortality, and focusing on making small but significant contributions.

Living a meaningful life is an often-discussed concept. In his essays, Seneca suggests that living a meaningful life requires embracing difficult moments and living with intention. He writes: *"If we want to reach the furthest limits of our potential, we must accept the challenges that life offers us."*

Perhaps one of the most important aspects of living a meaningful life is staying connected to your purpose. As Martin Luther King Jr. voiced, *"If you haven't discovered something that you will die for, then you aren't fit to live."* Having a clear sense of purpose helps us stay resilient, even when faced with difficult challenges and setbacks in life.

Being mindful of our habits also has an important role to play in living a meaningful life. Aristotle pointed out that we are what we repeatedly do, highlighting that habits shape who we become in our lives. For this reason, it is essential to develop and practice habits that align with our values.

To lead a meaningful life involves building strong relationships with those around us, be it family members or friends The Dalai Lama stated this beautifully when he said, *"Love and compassion are necessities, not luxuries; without them humanity cannot survive."* Connecting with people on an emotional level adds depth and richness to our lives. Cultivating meaningful relationships can be an immensely rewarding experience. However, there are some important steps to take to foster more fulfilling connections.

The first step is to learn how to become an active listener by genuinely engaging with the other person and attempting to understand their point of view. This can be achieved through expressing interest in the conversation and striving to build a strong connection through body language and thoughtful conversations.

It can also be helpful to show kindness and compassion when connecting with others as this will help create deeper bonds. Showing gratitude for people's time and openness, as well as offering support during difficult times, can go a long way in cultivating meaningful relationships.

Lastly, it is also important to dedicate enough time to these interactions. Taking part in shared activities, such as going for a walk or exploring new places together, is a great way of spending quality time with each other.

Living a meaningful life also means striving to make an impact in the world. Seneca wrote: *"No man can live happily who considers himself alone; for we are born for mutual assistance. And it is only when we actually help each other that we shall enjoy lasting comfort and security."* This suggests that relationships through which we gain support and understanding, as well as providing the same for others, provide us with greater purpose in life.

Choosing to embrace hardship and difficulty can also contribute to living a meaningful life. As Viktor Frankl said, *"Success in life cannot be measured by any external standard; it is measured by the spirit with which you undertake and continue your struggle."* Overcoming difficult moments in life requires resilience and determination. Rather than turning away from challenging times, it is important to embrace them and understand that they can bring opportunity for growth. Learning from difficult experiences helps us grow in wisdom and resilience, which adds value to our lives.

One way of doing this is by developing a positive outlook on life. Rather than focusing on the difficulties we face, pay attention to the small accomplishments and successes along the way that can help us stay motivated and hopeful for what is ahead. Having an appreciation for the small moments can help to make life more meaningful, as opposed to constantly trying for bigger or better achievements. Mother Teresa taught this when she said, *"Not all of us can do great things. But we can do small things with great love."*

It can also be helpful to practice self-care activities such as exercise, mindfulness, or spending time outdoors to foster a sense of peace and relaxation. Seeking support from family and friends when facing difficult times can be immensely helpful too. Cultivating meaningful relationships helps us to gain perspective on our own experiences while feeling loved and supported. In Helen Keller's words, *"Alone we can do so little; together we can do so much."*

Living a meaningful life requires staying connected with your purpose, practicing productive habits, connecting with others meaningfully with love and compassion, striving to make an impact on the world, and embracing challenges in life as opportunities for growth.

The Legacy of Your Actions

The legacy we leave behind is important in life since it reflects our values as individuals. Every action we take has an impact on others and can influence future generations. By recognising this, we can make decisions that will honour our beliefs and create a lasting impression that will continue even after we are gone.

Life is short and full of unexpected twists and turns that can leave us feeling vulnerable and powerless. We may not be able to control our circumstances or predict the future, but we do have the choice to shape our lives through our actions. Fear and passivity can lead to a life without legacy if you choose to act out of fear or use your time inefficiently. Fear can cause you to make decisions based on what you want to avoid instead of what you should do, leading you into a life of inaction with no lasting legacy. Passivity can also hinder progress toward an intentional legacy as it breeds complacency and prevents you from taking meaningful action. Both fear and passivity can create an environment in which your choices are dictated by external forces, rather than conscious decision-making that would otherwise contribute to an intentional legacy.

It's true that we will all eventually die, but until then, how we live is the most powerful measure of our legacy. Every decision and action taken today contributes in some way to what we leave behind tomorrow. To quote Henry David Thoreau, *"Our life is frittered away by detail... Simplify, simplify!"* By living a life that aligns with purposeful values and priorities, rather than one influenced by fear and external influences, each of us can create a lasting impact that far outlasts our presence on this Earth.

Roman philosopher Cicero also promoted this idea when he said, *"Time makes ruins of all things; since it crumbles strong walls into dust, overthrows cities and nations alike, causes royal palaces to sink down into oblivion; yet there are some things which no lapse of time can efface: good deeds endure forever."* Our actions reflect our character and become part of the fabric of history – whether for better or worse – so it's important that each of us strive to be purposeful in the choices we make.

Seneca summed up this concept in saying, *"As long as you live, keep learning how to live."* By learning about ourselves and striving for personal growth each day, imbuing each action with virtue and integrity, we have the capacity to make an impact beyond anything imaginable now, thereby leaving behind more than just memories or stories – leaving behind a legacy worth remembering.

We must remember that every choice we make has a lasting effect, and it's up to us to ensure that our future legacy is one of meaning rather than regret. Our lives may be finite, but with each passing moment, the decisions we make can together form a bigger picture, or an intentional legacy of our actions. As Plato wrote: *"The beginning is the most important part of the work."* We can choose to live deliberately, and focus on being conscious of our choices and how they affect us in the long term.

When faced with a choice or difficult decision, ask yourself, "If I do this now, what kind of legacy will I leave behind?" Taking the time to reflect on this could help you stay true to your values, consider consequences more carefully, and ultimately lead to more meaningful choices and outcomes. Every action taken today shapes the future. By being mindful of this fact, our decisions today can inspire positive change for generations to come. *Be the change you wish to see in the world.*

The choices we make shape our character and become part of history. Martin Luther King Jr once said, *"The time is always right to do what is right."* By living a life of purpose and good intentions, rather than one influenced by fear or passivity, each of us can create a lasting impact and legacy that far outlasts our presence on this Earth.

It's up to us to choose how we want to be remembered. Our lives may only be short, but with each passing moment, the decisions we make can together form a bigger picture; an intentional legacy of our actions. Every action taken today shapes the future; mindfulness of this fact could help us stay true to our values and lead to more meaningful outcomes for those who follow us.

Living a life of intention is an important part of creating a legacy that has lasting impact. In Seneca's words, *"It's not that we have so little time but that we lose so much."* Our decisions and actions can shape our character, define who we are, and become our part in history. Doing what is right is using our time well to create something meaningful, rather than allowing fear or passivity to influence us. By making conscious decisions today, we can leave an intentional legacy behind, long after we are gone.

To summarise how you can create a lasting legacy through intentional action:

1. Recognise that every decision you make today has an effect on future generations, either for better or worse.
2. Live a life of purpose, with good intentions and values that you want to be remembered by.
3. Make mindful decisions based on what is right, rather than succumbing to fear or passivity.
4. Use your time wisely and intentionally: each action today shapes the future in some way.

5. Create something meaningful that will outlast your presence and leave behind an intentional legacy worth remembering.

Achieving Your Goals and Conquering Fear

We all strive to achieve our goals, but often we are faced with the daunting challenge of conquering our fears. All too often, fear holds us back from taking risks and pursuing our dreams. But, as motivational speaker Stephen Covey once said, *"The key is not to prioritise what's on your schedule, but to schedule your priorities."* We must take a step back and focus on the positives of achieving our goals, meaning the rewards that come with working hard and overcoming any obstacles in our paths.

To reach success, it is crucial that we have faith in ourselves. Writing for *Entrepreneur Magazine*, Eric Ries pointed out, *"There are no guarantees in life – only possibilities. If you get caught up in worrying about how long something will take or how it might fail, then you start down a slippery slope of pessimism; instead believe – really believe – in yourself and your skills enough to take the plunge into uncharted waters!"* Having self-confidence is one of the most crucial elements for achieving success. Without it, we won't be able to face our fears head on and push ourselves out of our comfort zone.

The importance of setting achievable goals has never been truer than today in a world where everything moves at lightning speed and distractions abound at every corner. However, if you can look deep within yourself and focus your energy on making progress toward your ambitions, anything is possible. Greek philosopher Epictetus once said, *"First say to yourself what you would be; and then do what you have to do."* In light of this timeless advice, let us make sure each day counts by getting rid of fear- inducing thoughts and focusing instead on the positive outcomes associated with working toward reaching those goals.

Economist John Maynard Keynes added to this line of thought by saying, *"The difficulty lies not so much in developing new ideas as in escaping from old ones."* It's easy to get comfortable with the status quo, but without a strong desire for change and self-belief in the abilities to accomplish the task at hand, our dreams will remain just that: dreams. We must stay focused, take risks, and march toward our goals with conviction to achieve anything worthwhile.

No matter how difficult a task may appear or how challenging it has become to stay on course, if we have faith, keep pushing forward, and strive each day for success, eventually all our efforts will pay off. As Mark Twain once commented, *"Twenty years from now, you will be more disappointed by the things that you didn't do than by the ones you did do."* Focusing on your goals with passion is one of the most rewarding experiences you can ever have. Life is short, and time passes quickly, so pursue what you want without hesitation and be victorious!

To stay focused and make consistent strides toward achieving success, it is important to break down your goals into smaller manageable chunks. This way, you gain a better understanding of what needs to be done daily and take action accordingly. Additionally, setting realistic expectations will go a long way in terms of ensuring you can keep yourself motivated and energised throughout the journey.

It is also important to cultivate optimism and look at setbacks as opportunities to learn rather than moments of defeat. Surround yourself with people who share similar goals and ideals to you. This will provide moral support as well as much needed inspiration during dark times. As Epictetus said, *"We have two ears and one mouth so that we can listen twice as much as we speak."* This is good advice that we should all take. Focus your energy on listening, learning, and strategizing how you will achieve success.

To overcome old ideas and keep yourself motivated, it is important to devise creative strategies and remain open-minded. Instead of relying on what has worked in the past, challenge yourself to come up with new approaches that have not been tried before. Consider brainstorming sessions where you can invite other people to share their unique perspectives and provide insights into different solutions.

You can also stay inspired by taking a break from your everyday routine and engaging in activities such as reading books, attending conferences, or volunteering for causes that are aligned with your goals. Additionally, using visualisation techniques can help with breaking away from ideas that no longer serve us, allowing new possibilities to enter our minds. As Thomas Edison once said, *"Vision without execution is just hallucination."* Make sure to take concrete steps toward making your dreams become reality!

Visualisation techniques are a powerful way to activate our subconscious mind and focus on the desired outcomes. To benefit from visualisation, try to create a mental picture of what you want to achieve. Use vivid details and try to engage all your senses. For example, imagine yourself achieving success: see the look of accomplishment on your face, feel the sense of pride and joy as you celebrate with others, smell success in the air, hear your heart pounding in anticipation, and taste the fruit of victory on your lips. Once this image is strongly anchored in your mind, take some time each day to revisit it and reinforce it. This will help create an emotional connection that will keep you motivated, even when progress feels slow or when obstacles seem too big. With consistent practice, visualisation can become second nature and help you stay focused on your goals.

To reach a meaningful conclusion in life, it's essential to have goals that you can strive toward with courage and dedication. Along the way, there will be moments of uncertainty when fear might stop you from pursuing your ambitions. However, if you can push through these moments by embracing challenges with determination, then you will succeed. So, visualise your success, conquer your fears, have faith in yourself, set achievable goals, take breaks, and stay focused with optimism and creativity.

Making Difficult Decisions

Life presents us with some tough choices from time to time and although making difficult decisions may feel uncomfortable, it is a key element of reaching a meaningful conclusion in life because it forces us to examine our values closely. By doing so, we can make decisions based on what is truly important to us in that moment instead of defaulting to something easier or more comfortable.

Making difficult decisions is one of the most trying and challenging tasks a person can face in life. It takes courage, strength of character, and clarity of reasoning. Seneca argued that every choice should be weighed carefully. Difficult decisions can also prompt fear and uncertainty as they require us to make concessions and put our trust in something new.

In the words of Confucius, *"The superior man understands what is right; the inferior man understands what will sell."* Making difficult decisions should not just consider profitability or convenience, it should always consider facts, morals, and ethics for long-term sustainability. Difficult decisions involve taking calculated risks, but often require intense thought before action can be taken.

Martin Luther King Jr once said, *"We must accept finite disappointment, but never lose infinite hope."* Although making difficult decisions can mean failure and disappointment along the way, it also opens up different possibilities that may ultimately lead us to a better future. This is why it's important to have faith and remain open-minded when taking on new challenges or unfamiliar territories, as it will help to make difficult decisions with confidence. Difficult decisions require thinking through consequences thoroughly to make wise choices for yourself and those around you in the long term.

When making difficult decisions, weigh the pros and cons of each path to make an informed decision. The pros of a particular decision may include greater personal satisfaction or financial gain, while the cons could be risks associated with unfamiliarity as well as potential failure. On the other hand, opting for a less popular course of action may bring with it unexpected rewards yet carry greater unpredictable risks. In either case, a diligent assessment of both possibilities should be made to identify any hidden traps or unknown benefits so that the best possible outcome can be achieved.

Although making difficult decisions can be a challenge, there are many strategies to make the process easier. These include taking the time to assess both options without rushing, seeking advice from trusted sources such as friends or family members, writing down all relevant pros and cons of each option to gain clarity, and imagining how different outcomes may be beneficial or harmful. Additionally, understanding your own values and priorities can help you in making your decision. The goal of any decision-making practice should be to ensure that the results are satisfactory now and in the future.

Decisions should be based on your values, facts, morals, and ethics. Weigh up the pros and cons, considering priorities and consequences, and aim to achieve the best possible outcomes.

Striving for Fulfilment and Greatness

While reaching goals brings fulfilment, striving for greatness pushes us beyond what was previously thought possible, enabling us to not only complete tasks but excel in them by setting higher expectations. Achievement then provides a greater sense of satisfaction, and takes us closer to the meaningful conclusion we seek in life.

Life is short, yet we are capable of so much. Striving for greatness and fulfilment are key tenets that can help us make the most of our lives. This doesn't mean that life should be a constant struggle against your own limitations. It's important to take breaks, rest, and relax even when you're striving for something bigger. Striving for greatness isn't about outdoing others or competing with your peers. True greatness lies in self-improvement and self-awareness.

There are many ways to challenge yourself to strive for greatness. Firstly, it is important to be aware of your own strengths and weaknesses and use them to set achievable goals. This allows you to take on challenges that push beyond your comfort zone and help you grow both inside and out. Create achievable targets over time rather than trying to do everything at once. Achievable goals are motivating since small successes are achieved along the way with the overarching objective always visible. This method can be augmented by finding mentors or coaches who have experience of the same journey and can provide valuable insights on how best to strive for greatness.

Keep sight of the bigger picture instead of being overwhelmed with individual tasks. It's difficult to stay focused on what you're striving for if you become bogged down in the details. As Confucius said, *"It does not matter how slow you go, as long as you do not stop."* Take your time and make intentional decisions that will help you reach your ultimate goal faster.

Striving for greatness isn't always about hard work. Taking breaks, resting, and relaxing when needed are essential for maintaining balance within yourself and ensuring you are physically and mentally able to take on new tasks. In the words of Henry Ford, *"If everyone is moving forward together, then success takes care of itself."*

Take part in activities outside your usual routine to broaden your perspective and get a more holistic view of the world. This may include trying new hobbies, exploring different cultures, meeting new people, or learning new skills. All these activities can provide invaluable insights for challenging yourself.

Adopting an open mindset and being comfortable with taking risks are also key factors when striving for greatness. Stepping outside your comfort zone brings you closer to success as you explore unknown territory. It's important not to become disillusioned by fear or doubt, and to maintain a positive attitude while accepting challenges as they come.

Understanding failure helps us learn from our mistakes rather than being ashamed of them or withering away in fear because of them. Mistakes and failures can often be the best way to challenge yourself to grow and achieve more. As Maya Angelou once said, *"Be as proud of yourself when you fail as when you succeed."*

Finally, increased knowledge should be seen as an essential tool when striving for greatness. Reading books, attending seminars, or participating in workshops related to your goals are sources of valuable advice from experts that can help accelerate the process of achieving excellence!

In summary, true greatness lies in self-awareness and self-improvement. Keep sight of the bigger picture, set achievable targets, take breaks, try new activities, take risks outside your comfort zone, accept failures as learning points, and strive to learn new knowledge.

Living Beyond Ambition, Power, and Wealth

Although ambition, power, and wealth all serve as motivators, living solely based on these concepts does not lead to a meaningful conclusion. These things do not address deeper desires such as acceptance, or understanding deeper needs like love and companionship, which lead to greater feelings of security and stability. These aid true long-term fulfilment, rather than short-term gratification based on superficial successes and achievements.

We often hear about the importance of ambition, power, and wealth in our pursuit of happiness and success.

However, these goals can be limiting if we focus too much on them alone. Seneca believed, *"We waste our lives striving after things which will make us no happier when gained than they did while they were still being sought by us."*

Living beyond ambition, power, and wealth means recognising that there is more to life than what can be measured or bought with money. It involves understanding that true satisfaction comes from finding meaning in everyday moments and creating valuable connections with others. As Gandhi said, *"Happiness is when what you think, what you say, and what you do are in harmony."*

Another important part of living beyond ambition, power, and wealth is valuing experiences over material objects. Experiences like travelling to new places or attending cultural events can enrich your life beyond measure. Studies have shown that spending money on experiences rather than objects makes people happier in the long run. A 2006 study conducted by psychologists at Cornell University found that participants experienced much higher levels of life satisfaction when they spent money on leisure activities and experiential purchases rather than material goods. Another 2012 survey conducted by Harris Interactive found that Americans who spent money on a memorable experience, such as a vacation, reported feeling significantly happier than those who purchased items such as clothes or jewellery. In Benjamin Franklin's words, *"Money spent for a thing gives it value; spent for an experience gives us memories to keep forever."*

Knowing how to find joy outside of economic measurement requires looking inward with introspection and contemplation. Having meaningful pursuits outside money-based objectives can give us fulfilment on a level that goes deeper than achieving conventional measures of success. Make time for activities that bring personal fulfilment, such as reading a book or attending a cultural event. Spend your money on experiences rather than objects as studies have shown that this can make you happier in the long run. Live simply and savour life's simple pleasures. Remember that happiness is found in harmony between what you think, say, and do, not exclusively in any one measure of success.

There are many things in life that are important outside of ambition, power, and wealth objectives. Everyone has differing priorities, and trying to define what is important to someone can be difficult. Here are some examples of other things of importance:

- Enjoying quality time with friends and family
- Creating meaningful relationships
- Living a healthy lifestyle
- Engaging in creative activities
- Being kind to yourself and others
- Fostering an appreciation for nature
- Pursuing passions or hobbies
- Giving back to the community
- Finding joy in simple pleasures

Living beyond ambition, power, and wealth is about understanding that true satisfaction comes from more than just material gain. It involves appreciating everyday moments, creating meaningful connections with others, valuing experiences over objects, and reflecting on what truly brings lasting joy.

Learning the Value of Friendship and Family

Friendships and familial bonds are the strongest connections humans have. Friends provide support regardless of changing circumstances over time, and they provide camaraderie and perspective from peers. Familial bonds offer strong foundations and cultural ties. With friends and family, you can reach further than your individual efforts could ever achieve alone.

Seneca understood the importance of relationships, especially those between friends and family. He noted: *"We can only live in harmony with others when we understand our true place in society."* To him, friendship was essential to understand our collective humanity and realise our full potential in life. By understanding our connection to others, we can come together for mutual benefit and realise that our lives don't need to be lived in isolation.

This idea has been echoed by thought leaders throughout history. Buddha believed that human relationships are complex and always evolving, presenting us with an ever-changing spectrum of learning opportunities. Confucius emphasised that virtuous behaviour toward friends was an essential component of his philosophy, and one that should be cultivated at all times to achieve true personal growth and development. And Friedrich Nietzsche argued that meaningful friendships were not just beneficial but essential to experience lasting fulfilment throughout life's journey.

These values still hold true today. Friendship and family remain vital components of a fulfilling life, no matter how short it may be. Our relationships provide us with emotional nourishment, support us when we need it most, and challenge us on different levels so that we can become better versions of ourselves.

Research shows that meaningful relationships are beneficial for both physical and mental health outcomes. A study published in *Nature Communications* found that people who had good social connections with family, friends, and community members experienced improved immune system functioning and better overall cardiovascular health. Friendship has also been linked to decreased levels of stress, improved psychological wellbeing, increased self-esteem, and higher levels of happiness.

Meaningful relationships with family, friends, neighbours, colleagues, or mentors can provide us with social support that is essential for our mental wellbeing. Social support helps us cope with difficult emotions such as anxiety or depression, gives us someone to rely on during times of crisis, provides guidance when making important decisions, boosts self-confidence, and encourages healthy lifestyle changes by providing accountability.

Strong relationships bring joy into our lives through shared experiences ranging from simple conversations over coffee to more exciting adventures like going on vacation together or pursuing hobbies side by side.

Having people in your life who understand you emotionally can be immensely comforting and help you find purpose in life, something we all strive for at one point or another.

Building meaningful relationships with family and friends can be a challenging but worthwhile endeavour. Here are some tips to help you cultivate stronger connections:

- Communicate openly and honestly with your loved ones. Listen actively when they speak and be open to expressing your opinions, ideas, struggles, and experiences.
- Be available for one another even when life gets busy. Schedule weekly or monthly activities that bring you all closer together such as movie nights, game nights, or dinners.
- Establish boundaries so that everyone feels respected and heard. Respect other people's opinions and feelings, while also taking care of yourself emotionally.
- Celebrate special moments such as birthdays and anniversaries, or simply take time to acknowledge the daily joys in life together.
- Show vulnerability by opening up about what's going on in your life. This is an important part of building trust with one another.
- Invest in shared experiences like attending live events, volunteering together, or learning something new side by side.
- Offer words of encouragement often. Telling someone how much they mean to you or what qualities you admire about them will make a difference in deepening the connection between you.

ROBERT N. JACOBS

Here are some activities you can use to help foster strong relationships with family and friends:

- Start a book club or movie night, where everyone can come together in a safe environment to discuss books, movies, and share ideas.
- Join a community sports team or enrol in a fitness class together. Physical activity is a great way to bond.
- Take regular weekend trips or day trips to explore new places with your loved ones.
- Have game nights, where everyone can come together for board games and friendly competition.
- Host potlucks wherein each person brings their favourite dish to share. It's an opportunity for good food and meaningful conversations!
- Organise creative projects such as painting classes or music jam sessions. Creating something together is always fun.

Friendship and family are vital components of a fulfilling life, beneficial to physical and mental health, providing social support, and bringing joy. So, work hard to build relationships, maintain communication with loved ones, give them time, and share experiences such as hobbies, daytrips, holidays, or just a simple meal together.

Death as Part of Life's Journey

Death is an ever-present reality in life's journey and understanding it can provide valuable perspective. In Seneca's words, *"The longest-lived and the shortest-lived of us are impermanent."* This simple phrase captures the essential truth that everyone, regardless of their life span, will experience death at some point.

Death is a fact of life, but it doesn't have to be feared. Rather than viewing death as a negative outcome, it can be seen as part of the natural cycle of life. When we recognise this inevitability and accept it as part of our journey, we can live with greater appreciation for the things that do matter in life, or as Alan Cohen put it, *"Death reminds us how much life means."*

The concept of death can help us to grow as individuals by pushing us out of our comfort zones and into situations where we have to take risks and push past our limitations, learning new things along the way. Facing death can also make us more aware of how precious life is, which can motivate us to seize every opportunity that comes our way and make sure that it counts toward something meaningful.

We don't get to choose how we die, but we can choose how we live now. This emphasises the importance of using death as a reminder that life is finite and should be lived to its fullest extent. In this way, the concept of death becomes a tool for making positive changes within ourselves instead of something that serves only as a source of fear or despair.

One practical example of how death can be a tool for positive change is in the way that it can help us to become more self-aware and live life with intention. By being mindful of our mortality, we can learn to appreciate the beauty in living for today rather than worrying about tomorrow. This attitude can help us to become more present and aware of our thoughts and feelings as well as be more intentional with the time we have left.

Accepting the inevitability of death can provide us with valuable insight into what is truly important in life. Instead of chasing after material possessions or outward success, we can choose to focus on aspects that really matter such as relationships with family and friends, experiences that bring joy, and pursuits that leave a lasting impact. In this way, acceptance serves as an enlightening reminder that life is short and should be enjoyed while it lasts.

Though death may be unavoidable, there are ways to make sure our lives continue to have meaning even after we die. One way is by leaving behind meaningful legacies – works or deeds that will live on after our physical bodies are gone. The motivation behind creating such legacies was articulated eloquently by Ernest Becker when he said, *"Man's concern is to insure his being against oblivion, to establish himself and maintain himself eternally in being. He needs a symbolic immortality; he must have something protecting him from the threat of annihilation always present in the consciousness of finiteness and mortality."*

In other words, death gives us the opportunity to make our mark on the world with what we create before passing away. It's important not to procrastinate because any day could be our last one, something Seneca reminded us of in saying, *"All human affairs form a continuous chain; for things following each other no man can assign a limit beforehand; yet all these future events exist in the mind of nature even now, though they reveal themselves at their proper time only."* With this in mind, let's make sure to fill whatever days we have left with intentionality and purpose!

To create a lasting legacy while still alive, it's important to make sure that whatever you do reflects the values and aspirations you hold closest to your heart. Taking time each day to reflect on what matters most to you will help keep your life purposeful and meaningful.

Developing meaningful relationships with those around you is another way to leave a lasting impression. By connecting with people in an authentic and genuine way, you can turn acquaintances into lasting friendships that can benefit both parties well beyond the physical presence of either one.

Making sure that your work leaves something behind that will outlast you is also key for leaving a lasting legacy. Whether it's through music, art, or writing, creating meaningful works will ensure that your impact lives on even after your physical form has left this world. In the words of Paulo Coelho, *"When the soul leaves its body, nothing is lost; everything continues."*

Using your resources to contribute toward causes greater than yourself is another excellent way to create a lasting legacy while still alive. When we give back without expecting anything in return, we are showing our gratitude to those who have helped us along the way, while ensuring that our efforts live on far longer than ourselves.

In summary, facing the concept of death is a powerful motivator for taking action toward meaningful goals. Rather than getting caught up in trivial matters, facing our mortality helps us recognise that time is limited, and every moment counts. This recognition can fill us with determination to make the most of life by turning dreams into reality before it's too late.

Your Legacy to Others

Many of us think about our life as if it were an expansive river, winding its way through the ages with no end in sight. But life is not like that at all. Throughout history, great minds have taught us that taking responsibility for our legacy should be a fundamental part of our life plan.

When we take full ownership of our legacy, we embrace risk and uncertainty and strive to make the best decisions possible in each moment. We acknowledge that every decision has consequences and understand that failure is an inherent part of success. Rather than relying solely on luck or outside influences to carry us through, we work hard to ensure that our actions lead us toward achieving whatever goals define our greater purpose in life.

Seneca learned this lesson well and lived by example regarding the importance of leaving a lasting impression. He said, *"We must look around at those who have gone before us and make sure we do not lag behind them; it gives much pleasure to exceed them; but there is nevertheless one thing which they leave with us, something they take with them only too often forgotten - their memory... It is essential that one's achievements should survive him; then he has built something which will bring him honour after he dies...one's name should be remembered not only during his lifetime but also afterwards."* This lesson has been taught in many ways throughout the centuries. Another example is found in Proverbs 22:1 (King James Version of the Bible): *"A good name is more desirable than great riches; to be esteemed is better than silver or gold."*

Taking personal accountability for your legacy doesn't mean trying to become famous or having grandiose aspirations, it means understanding your own individual purpose in life and striving diligently toward fulfilling it, no matter how small the task may seem. Legacy isn't about power or fame, it's about leading with purpose and bringing meaningful change into this world through lasting impact and deeds done today so that future generations can benefit from them tomorrow.

One of the most inspiring examples of people who have left a positive legacy is Nelson Mandela. He is renowned for his powerful anti-apartheid leadership and dedication to social justice, freedom, and human rights. Through these commitments, he helped unite a diverse nation and become one of the most revered political activists of all time.

Another example is Malala Yousafzai. At only 18, she became the youngest Nobel Prize laureate in history due to her unwavering commitment to girls' education throughout the world. Her courage and determination have earned her widespread respect from around the globe and continue to be an inspiration for future generations.

A further example is Mother Teresa's dedication to serving the poorest members of society with love and compassion. She created a worldwide network of charitable organisations designed to uplift those living in extreme poverty, earning her a Nobel Peace Prize in 1979 for her humanitarian work. Even after her death, Mother Teresa's lasting impact continues to inspire individuals from all walks of life.

Mahatma Gandhi is perhaps one of the most memorable examples of someone leaving a positive legacy. He changed the course of history through his nonviolent protest movement against British colonial rule in India, ultimately leading to independence for his nation. His commitment to peaceful activism serves as an inspiration to this day.

Rosa Parks is also remembered for her refusal to give up her seat on a segregated bus in 1955, an act at the heart of the civil rights movement in the US. Her courage and bravery spark meaningful discussions about racism and social justice even today.

The life of Martin Luther King Jr. was also defined by his legacy of standing up for civil rights and striving toward a more equitable society. Through his passionate speeches and nonviolent protests, he not only improved conditions for African Americans, but also set an example that continues to resonate with people around the world decades later.

Taking responsibility for your legacy to others should be a fundamental part of your life plan, so work hard to ensure that your actions lead you toward achieving whatever goals define your greater purpose in life.

A Meaningful and Fulfilled Life

To reach a meaningful conclusion in life, you need to look beyond material possessions such as money, fame, or power and instead focus on giving and offering personal value that benefits society and the environment at large. Reaching a meaningful conclusion in life can be one of the most difficult challenges you ever face. It requires a combination of contemplation, introspection, and courage to truly come to terms with the reality of your existence. In what is perhaps Seneca's most famous quote, he wrote: *"It is not that we have a short time to live, but that we waste a lot of it. Life is long enough, and a sufficiently generous amount has been given to us for the highest achievements if it were all well invested. But when it is wasted in heedless luxury and spent on no good activity, we are forced at last by death's final constraint to realise that it has passed away before we knew it was passing. So it is: we are not given a short life, but we make it short, and we are not ill-supplied but wasteful of it... Life is long if you know how to use it."*

With these words, Seneca emphasises the importance of making the most of our time in this world. He is far from alone in this regard, as there are many other thought leaders who have shared insights on how to make the most of life's brevity. For example, Henry David Thoreau said, *"The price of anything is the amount of life you exchange for it,"* reflecting on how important it is to prioritise what really matters when making decisions about how to spend your limited time wisely.

Living a meaningful life also means understanding what death brings us, namely an awareness that all things must eventually come to an end, and an appreciation of the time spent while alive. Writer Albert Camus stated, *"In any case after a certain point, death could be seen not as extinction but as fulfilment."*

Reaching a meaningful conclusion in life requires dedication and commitment. It is important to remember that each person's journey is unique, so it is best to create goals and objectives that are tailored to individual needs and circumstances.

The first step in creating a plan for reaching a meaningful conclusion in life is to set aside time for reflection and introspection. Taking the time to think about what matters most and what can be done with the remaining time in this world is essential for any meaningful journey. It also helps to take into consideration the words of Seneca, Thoreau, Camus, and other thought leaders who have shared their insights on how to make the most of life's brevity.

The next step is to create realistic goals by prioritising the activities worth pursuing, and leaving the rest behind.

Once these goals have been set, it is important to take action toward achieving them. This could mean practical steps like organising your finances, doing volunteer work, or gaining new skills, as well as more existential steps such as cultivating relationships with family and friends, or engaging in religious or spiritual pursuits.

Finally, it is important to balance your life in terms of material achievements alongside intangibles like self-reflection, contemplation, and moments of joy. Balance is essential if a life of meaning is to be lived before reaching its conclusion.

Thinking about reaching a meaningful conclusion in life can be a daunting prospect, especially if faced with adversity or complex circumstances. However, by contemplating your mortality and considering how best to use your remaining days on Earth, it may become easier to determine which actions are worth taking and which might be likely to lead you astray. Take time for reflection. Identify and prioritise your meaningful goals, and take action toward them while maintaining a balance between material achievements, self-reflection, contemplation, moments of joy, and what you can give to society in a broader sense. In this way, you can gain clarity on the type of life you want to live and how best to reach your ultimate destination: an appreciation of the essence of time, meaningful achievements, and a fulfilled life.

Concluding Summary

Living a meaningful life requires staying connected with your purpose, practicing productive habits, connecting with others meaningfully with love and compassion, striving to make an impact on the world, and embracing challenges in life as opportunities for growth.

Create a lasting legacy through intentional action:

1. Recognise that every decision you make today has an effect on future generations, either for better or worse.
2. Live a life of purpose with good intentions and values that you want to be remembered by.
3. Make mindful decisions based on what is right, rather than succumbing to fear or passivity.
4. Use your time wisely and intentionally. Each action today shapes the future in some way.
5. Create something meaningful that will outlast your presence and leave behind an intentional legacy worth remembering.

To reach a meaningful conclusion in life, it's essential to have goals that you can strive toward with courage and dedication. Along the way, there will be moments of uncertainty when fear might stop you from pursuing your ambitions. However, if you can push through these moments by embracing challenges with determination, then you will succeed. So, visualise your success, conquer your fears, have faith in yourself, set achievable goals, take breaks, and stay focused with optimism and creativity.

Make decisions based on your values, facts, morals, and ethics. Weigh up the pros and cons, considering priorities and consequences, and aim to achieve the best possible outcomes.

True greatness lies in self-awareness and self-improvement. Keep sight of the bigger picture, set achievable targets, take breaks, try new activities, take risks outside your comfort zone, accept failures as learning points, and strive to learn new knowledge.

Living beyond ambition, power, and wealth is about understanding that true satisfaction comes from more than just material gain. It involves appreciating everyday moments, creating meaningful connections with others, valuing experiences over objects, and reflecting on what truly brings lasting joy.

Friendship and family are vital components of a fulfilling life, beneficial to physical and mental health, providing social support, and bringing joy. Work hard to build relationships, maintain communication with loved ones, give them time, and share experiences such as hobbies, daytrips, holidays, or just a simple meal together.

Facing the concept of death is a powerful motivator for taking action toward meaningful goals. Rather than getting caught up in trivial matters, face your mortality to recognise that time is limited, and every moment counts. Make the most of life by turning dreams into reality before it's too late.

Taking responsibility for your legacy to others should be a fundamental part of your life plan, so work hard to ensure that your actions lead you toward achieving whatever goals define your greater purpose in life.

In conclusion, take time for reflection. Identify and prioritise your meaningful goals, and then take action toward them, while maintaining a balance between material achievements, self-reflection, contemplation, moments of joy, and what you can give to society in a broader sense. In this way, you can gain clarity on the type of life you want to live and how best to reach your ultimate destination: an appreciation of the essence of time, meaningful achievements, and a fulfilled life.

THE END

References

Tim Ferriss (2007). *The 4-Hour Workweek: Escape 9-5. Live Anywhere, and Join the New Rich.*

Seneca the Younger (Circa 65 AD). *Letters from a Stoic.*

Seneca the Younger (Circa 65 AD). *Letters on Ethics: To Lucilius.*

Seneca the Younger (Circa 65 AD). *Anger, Mercy, Revenge.*

Seneca the Younger (Circa 65 AD). *The Complete Tragedies, Volume 1 & 2.*

Seneca the Younger (Circa 65 AD). *Hardship and Happiness.*

Seneca the Younger (Circa 65 AD). *Natural Questions.*

Seneca the Younger (Circa 65 AD). *On the Shortness of Life.*

Dave Allen (2011). *Getting Things Done.*

Marcus Aurelius, (Circa 170 AD). *The Meditations.*

Henry David Thoreau (1854). *Walden.*

Nelson Mandela (1994). *Long Walk To Freedom.*

Paulo Coelho (1988). *The Alchemist.*

King Solomon (Circa 700 BC). *Proverbs 22:1.*

Benjamin Franklin (1785). *Poor Richard's Almanack.*

Stephen R. Covey (1989). *The 7 Habits of Highly Effective People.*

Greg McKeown (2014). *Essentialism: The Disciplined Pursuit of Less.*

We have made every effort to ensure the reliability of the sources cited. Despite this, if you come across any inconsistencies, we encourage you to get in touch with the author at info@theabundancementor.co.uk. Rest assured, we will promptly address these inaccuracies in our subsequent publication.

Disclaimer: This book is intended purely for your enjoyment. We strongly suggest that those dealing with mental or physical health issues always seek counsel from a specialist.

Books by the Author

1. *Aspire for Abundance. Conversations With My Teenage Daughter. Road Trip Through Iceland.*
   ISBN: 9781803810218

2. *Daily Reflections: 365 Days of Contemplation for Mind & Soul.*
   ISBN: 9781803811642

3. *The Lion Inside. A Girl's Guide On How To Get What They Want and Live An Abundant Life.*
   ISBN: 9781803813592

4. *Abundance For Kids. Short Stories To Shape Mindsets of Little Learners.*
   ISBN: 9781803814728

5. *Standing Out. The Necessity of Admirable Character In a World Facing Moral Erosion.*
   ISBN: 9781803817422

Milton Keynes UK
Ingram Content Group UK Ltd.
UKHW010813100324
439004UK00002B/12